IN THE STEPS
OF THE
CRUSADERS

IN THE STEPS

OF THE

CRUSADERS

TEXT
by
Régine PERNOUD
Curator of the Musée d'Histoire de France

PHOTOGRAPHS
by
Frédérique DURAN

HASTINGS HOUSE, PUBLISHERS
NEW YORK

CONSTABLE AND COMPANY LIMITED
LONDON

Translated from the French by
Margaret Case

A MODERNE EQUIVALENT of medieval geography would be not, of course, Mercator's globes and projection but the great international routes. From the 10th century to the end of the 13th, geography was considered as a form of dynamics and more as a science of movement than of space. The known world was furrowed with great roads, marked at intervals by cathedrals and sanctuaries, and, while all led to Rome, their true end was Jerusalem. For Jerusalem was the centre of the world and the homeland of all mankind, the root of the tree of Christendom, planted on the hill in the form of a skull. At a period when every believer was a possible pilgrim and a pilgrimage not only an act of ritual piety—as it still is, for instance, with Moslems—but a living symbol of an essential feature of Christian life, that is to say of the same transient nature, transfiguring like the Paschal feast and being an attempt to live in harmony with the rhythm of a higher existence, there was no Christian of East or West who had not made his way at least in spirit toward the Holy Land.

The first great pilgrim—he may be considered as a medieval figure because of the influence he was to exercise on the Middle Ages—was none other than St. Jerome. This hermit, who was at one and the same time the father of the most arduous of sciences—that of exegetical scholarship—and the most widely read of writers (St. Jerome's version of the Bible was the one used in the West until modern times), was also the promoter of the biggest travel ventures of all times. The sojourn he made in Syria and the desert of Chalcis, where the great man of letters, versed in classical literature from childhood, spent his life in prayer, manual work and the study of Hebrew; the journeys he made to Constantinople, Cyprus and Egypt; and the passionate ardor with which he set about rediscovering the original text of the Bible, which brought him into contact with the most celebrated rabbis of the period; all these roused the ardent interest of the society of Rome to whom he wrote a voluminous correspondence. His spiritual daughters, Paula and Eustochia, who studied Hebrew and followed the saint to the monasteries of Egypt and Cyprus, decided to found a convent at Bethlehem and were obliged to open not one but four to satisfy the requests of all those who were attracted, girls like Eustochia or widows like Paula, her mother, to the life of the cloister in the places where Jesus had lived.

The first hostels for pilgrims were thus created, for all monasteries took in travellers. At the death of St. Jerome in 420, there were more than three hundred religious establishments, churches and hostels. The Holy Land became the great Christian centre for Biblical studies and monastic life. As soon as persecution had ceased and believers were free to proclaim themselves as such, a link had formed between East and West through the continual ebb and flow of pilgrimages which brought to the shores of Palestine Spaniards, Bretons and Italians, and North African and Byzantine Christians.

Some of these pilgrims have left narratives of their journeys, the earliest of which date from the 5th century. The *Peregrinatio Silviae*, the work of a nun called Etheria, remains the most famous of these. The writer describes a whole organization, including priest-guides and a police system on the roads, robbers being many in the mountainous regions and deserts which had to be crossed. Pilgrims always set off in groups, but not purely for security reasons—the case is, indeed, the same today when one has merely to take the train to Lourdes. The groups stopped not only at the places which Jesus had visited but also at the sites mentionned in the Old Testament. Etheria climbed Mount Sinai on which stood a church and monastery. She passed Jacob's well and her pilgrimage, which took no less than three years and included all the holy towns of Judea and Galilee, came to an end only at Constantinople. For two centuries countless other pilgrims made similar journeys. It was at this period that many stories and legends of oriental saints spread through Europe, together with their relics, while the popes erected hostels and monasteries in the East. The Eastern and Western divisions of the Church lived together in harmony and were a constant source of mutual spiritual enrichment. Over and above their theological quarrels, their union seems to have thrived on the peaceful exchanges they were able to make in the land of Israel, the refuge of prayer and sanctification.

ALL THIS BURNING LIFE and movement was to come brutally to and end, however, within less than half a century. In the history of the Christian communities of the East, the Arab conquest had the effect, as wrote Pirennus, of a "cosmic cataclysm". A first alarm had shaken the Christian world in 614, when Jerusalem was captured and pillaged by the Persians. Heraclius, the emperor of Byzantium, had barely reconquered the Holy City and triumphally replaced the True Cross in the basilica of Constantine, when the Moslem hordes bore down on the city, leaving the same Heraclius, the hero of the Byzantine struggle against the Sassanids, utterly helpless in front of their overwhelming numbers. One after the other, Aleppo, Antioch, Jerusalem (defended for two years by the patriarch Sophonius), Caesarea, and finally the whole of Syria and Palestine fell into the hands of the Saracens whom the religion of Mahomet had stirred to passion for the holy cause. Five years had not passed after the fall of Jerusalem when, in its turn, Alexandria capitulated in 643, marking the ruin of Egypt and the end of ten centuries of an extremely brilliant—alternatively pagan and Christian—civilization. The Moslems were finally to be defeated only before the gates of Byzantium itself, in 718, and in the West under the walls of Poitiers, in 732. But a century had been enough for the Mediterranean to become a "Moslem lake" and the whole of the Near East an Arab empire, in which the former eastern Roman empire strove desperately at Constantinople to maintain the Cross against the Crescent. Heresy, of course, in the same manner as schism in later years, had opened up the way to the invaders by fostering the quarrels and disunion among the different Christian armies that prevented them from making a strong front against the Turks. Monophysites, Nestorians, Copts and other dissidents had weakened their resistance against the new unity of the Arab world.

From then on, the route was barred and bands of pilgrims were no longer to be seen on the roads of Palestine. To all appearance at least; for in reality nothing could entirely prevent Christians from going to the Holy Land nor remove the attraction it held for the followers of Jesus. Documents of pilgrims dating from as early as 772 have come down to us. An ardent and adventurous Anglo-Saxon, one Willibald, succeeded with a few companions in gaining Syria and Palestine by way of Cyprus, returning through Constantinople and Rome. This little band took no less than seven years to make the pilgrimage and the narrative of the sufferings the companions endured shows to how great an extent conditions had changed since the time when monasteries had flourished at Bethlehem and Jerusalem.

At the end of the 8th century, Charlemagne was to take up the cause of these dauntless pilgrims which nothing could discourage. He entered into negotiations with the caliph Harunal-Rashid, and a "Frankish protectorate" was set up in the Holy Land which has left traces up to the present day. On their return from Baghdad, his ambassadors gave into his keeping the keys of the Holy Sepulchre and the Standard of Jerusalem as symbols of the sovereignty over the Holy Sepulchre conceded by the caliph to the future emperor (he was to be anointed at Rome a month later). The basilicas and monasteries were rebuilt, some of them at least, and Charlemagne was even able to take possession of Haceldama, the Field of Blood, where he erected a basilica and hostel for pilgrims. From this time on, the convents and hostels of the Holy Places became one of the concerns of the western princes. All those who were able, serfs and seigneurs, made the pilgrimage which is still the most important of Christendom. Sometimes it was imposed as a penitence, and the terrible Count of Anjou, Fulk Nerra, was ordered to make the journey three times. Until the beginning of the 11th century, it remained a difficult though not impossible undertaking and the state of comparative peace generally guaranteed the security of both the person and goods of the pilgrim.

Things were suddenly to change again, however, in the first years of the 11th century, showing how precarious the order observed up till then had been, subject as it was to the whim of the least sultan. For no apparent reason, in 1009 the caliph Hakim, a cruel madman, ordered the Holy Sepulchre to be demolished and Christians to be driven out. Further ruins and massacres were to follow in rapid succession; together with the basilica of Golgotha an the Church of St. Mary Latin, the monasteries of Jerusalem were destroyed and their goods confiscated. The Christians of Syria and Palestine were ordered to wear a copper cross weighing ten pounds as a sign of infamy. Persecution was to stop around 1020 as suddenly as it had begun. A few years later, the caliph allowed the Holy Sepulchre to be rebuilt. Calm was restored. But in 1064, a new catactrophe occurred, endangering once more the Holy Places and pilgrims. The Seljuk Turks, who siezed Jerusalem as early as 1078, destroying all the churches of Asia Minor on their way, became the masters of the whole of the Middle East, including the greater part of Greece.

It was this last Moslem offensive that was to provoke the retort of the Crusades, though it would be impossible to account for the latter without the thousand-year-old tradition of the pilgrimage to the Holy Land. For it was no ideology nor vulgar thirst for conquest that sent the Crusaders off through Asia Minor. In reality they were no more than armed pilgrims setting out on the road of their forefathers.

THE CRUSADES ACTUALLY BEGAN in the heart of France. Clermont in the province of Auvergne was the focal point of the routes which radiated throughout Europe, over land and sea, hill and dale, to the rotunda of the Holy Sepulchre. The appeal sent out from Clermont was to shake the foundations of the civilization of the Middle Ages for several hundred years, changing people's lives not only because it sent many far from their homes, but also because its echo was to reawaken the old dialogue between East and West. The Crusades removed the barrier, rendering possible once more the exchanges without which both Europe and the East could lead only a spiritually impoverished existence. And the reply to the call was to exceed all expectation, not only that of the barons and prelates who, on the 27th of November, 1095, heard Urban II's appeal to leave all to deliver the tomb of Christ, but that of the pope himself. The Pontiff was in exile at the time, having been driven out of Rome by a usurper. Yet, regardless of his own distress, he did not hesitate to call his followers to the gravest undertaking to which a pastor of the Church had ever exposed Christendom.

Nothing now remains to indicate actual site where the Council of Clermont was held, athough local tradition maintains that the meetings took place on what is today Champ et Square. The last meeting, which terminated with the cry of *"Deus vult"*, may indeed have taken place in the open air. But a church still in existence today is much more closely connected with the Crusaders solemn taking up of arms. It was from the cathedral of Puy that Urban II, after celebrating a pontifical Mass on the previous 15th of August, sent out his letters calling bishops and cardinals to the council, and it was there that he most probably explained his plans to the man in whom he saw the spiritual leader of the expedition, Adhemar of Monteil, the bishop of Puy. The Crusades thus started out under the protection of this old basilica which was then the most venerated centre of pilgrimage in France. Though the spirit of the Crusades was essentially international, France was undoubtedly their geographical origin. The Saracens, indeed, called anything that was European, Frankish. The initiative of Urban II, a French pope, was to revive in a most unexpected manner the old Frankish protectorate of the Holy Places of Charlemagne's time.

A more imperative call to arms than the appeal made to Christians of good will at the Council of Clermont was never heard on earth, unless it be that of the great medieval epic poems, which are, in any case, contemporary with the First Crusade. The Crusaders were ordered to start out on the following 15th of August for Constantinople, on the extreme edge of Europe, whence they were to strike on toward Syria and Palestine. Until then their task was to make an army out of all those who were ready to wear the little scarlet woollen cross on their shoulders. At least a year was necessary for the recruitment, provisioning and financing of the expedition. The pope had not reached Italy, however, before popular preachers had begun to spread through Europe, addressing the crowds on the highways and at the big fairs. One of them was to rouse such immense enthusiasm and gather together such a large number of followers that very rapidly it was to him, Peter the Hermit, that the idea of the Crusade was attributed. He has become, indeed, in history as in legend, the living symbol of Christianity on the march.

The hermit's ardor as a preacher was even to exceed his original aim and to turn the flood of enthusiasm into a kind of popular rising. But the prestige enjoyed by this little man in a grey hood who, on his ass, went all over the north and centre of France from the plains of Picardy to the province of Berry, was not enough to persuade the people to wait until the official starting date. An unruly throng set out ahead of the regular army and all kinds of unexpected incidents were to happen outside the prescriptions of the true leaders.

The Crusade proper started out, as arranged, toward the 15th of August, 1096. To facilitate supplies, the various sections were to make their way through Europe separately and to meet at Constantinople.

The first group consisted mainly of Walloon Crusaders from part of present-day Belgium and the French border. It was their chief who was to become the hero of the Crusade, personifying, like St. Louis in later years, the truly chivalrous knight. His courage, generosity, sincere piety and unselfishness won the confidence of all and made him the natural arbitrator in the various disputes that could not fail to break out among the ever turbulent barons from all over Europe, each accustomed to being independent, each with his own personality, and, in spite of the good will of most, with the shortcomings of his race, which were to become only more marked in the ensuing quarrels over booty.

Godfrey of Bouillon was the duke of Lower Lorraine, later the duchy of Brabant. The Castle of Bouillon after which he was named was in the heart of Wallonia, though Godfrey was born at Boulogne. His two brothers, Baldwin, later king of Jerusalem, and Eustacei count of Boulogne, together with their cousin, Baldwin of Burg, accompanied Bouillon. The counts of Hainault, Toul, Stenay and Stavelot were also members of their group. They made their way across the Holy Roman Empire, down the valley of the Danube, into Hungary, where Godfrey of Bouillon spoke with the king of Hungary, Coloman, on the bridge of Oedenburg, leaving his brother Baldwin as a hostage. His army was thus able to get to Semlin without difficulty. From there, taking exactly the same way as Peter the Hermit, Godfrey made for Belgrade. Halfway between Belgrade and Nish, he was met by the envoys of Alexis Comnenus. The emperor promised to supply the Crusaders with provisions if they gave their word not to pillage. After exchanging pledges, Godfrey's army was able to go on, by way of Nish, Philippopoli and Andrianople, to the shores of the Sea of Marmara halting at Selymbria, where it probably arrived on the 12th of December, 1096. Difficulties now began to be made by the Byzantine emperor, who claimed for himself all the lands the Crusaders might conquer. The same difficulties were to arise periodically throughout the history of the Crusades, compromising to a great extent their results and bringing about the fall of Constantinople four centuries later, after that of the Latin kingdoms of the East. The troops of Godfrey were finally billetted in the suburbs of Petra, before being sent to the coast of Asia, west of Nicomedia, not far from the place where the Popular Crusade had met its fate.

MEANWHILE, ANOTHER ARMY formed of Crusaders from Provence had set out. This second group may be considered as the core of the Crusade, since Adhemar of Monteil, the bishop of Puy and spiritual director of the enterprise, and the papal legate journeyed with it. The many knights of the group, whose names are full of the savor of the poetry of their native Languedoc, included Rambald of Orange, Gerard of Roussillon, William of Montpellier, etc..., under the direction of the Count of Toulouse himself, Raymund of Saint Gilles. The latter, the most powerful nobleman of the south of France, if not of all France (the estates of the king himself being at this period tiny in comparison with the rich southern domains over which Saint Gilles ruled) had made the vow never to return to his homeland.

The knights of Provence started out by way of northern Italy, Istria, Croatia and the Dalmatian coast. They stopped at Ragusa (today Dubrounik), Scutari and Durazzo and from there took the road to Macedonia through Pelargonia, Ostrovo and Wodena. They crossed parts of Greece which were later to become fiefs of the Frankish knights : Salonika, Serres, Kavala and Christopolis. Several skirmishes occurred with the unfriendly population and Adhemar of Monteil even had to remain some time at Salonika to recover from wounds he had received during an attack by Petcheneg horsemen—who were in the pay of the Byzantine emperor. Thus, although on empire territory, the Crusaders met with hostility on the part of the population. To such an extent that, after their arrival at Rossa (Keshan), which they carried by storm, the imperial troops retaliated a few days later, by siezing Rodosto, which was in the hands of the army of Provence. Only the pacifying genius of Godfrey of Bouillon could calm Raymund of Saint Gilles when the latter arrived at Constantinople.

In the meantime, a third, rather more unexpected army had set out. This group consisted of the Normans of Italy who, under the leadership of Robert Guiscard, had recaptured Sicily from the Saracens and to whom any expedition in the Orient was a most tempting adventure. The son of Robert Guiscard, Bohemund, was laying siege to the town of Amalfi, which had revolted, when he heard of the great events prepared by the pope. It was an ideal opportunity for him to conquer the lands he had already attempted to sieze in Greece and the Balkans. So he took the cross with his nephew, Tancred, and a number of Norman knights, his companions. In the month of November, 1096, this unexpected reinforcement landed on the coast of Albania, at Avlona, and made its way through the north of Greece (Kastoria, Ostrovo and Serres) to Thrace and Constantinople.

One last French group was to arrive on the shores of the Bosporus. Led by the son of William the Conqueror, Robert Courteheuse, it had crossed Italy and sailed from Brindisi to Durazzo on the Dalmatian coast. From there, like the other groups, it had taken the via Egnatia, the old Roman way which went through Ochrida, Ostrovo and Vodena to Salonika. The final march to Constantinople was made by the usual route, passing Kavala, Rodosto and Selymbria.

AFTER JOINING FORCES AT CONSTANTINOPLE, where the difficulties with Alexis were to go on for some time yet, the Crusaders concentrated around Nicomedia, the last stronghold in the region still belonging to the Byzantine Empire. While the supplies necessary for the next part of the expedition were got together, Godfrey of Bouillon cleared the road from Nicomedia to Nicaea, the first stronghold on the Crusaders' route occupied by the Turks. It was there that, on the 6th of May, 1097, the Crusaders found themselves for the first time face to face with those they had come to fight. The siege was to last over a month and finished with the Franks taking the city by storm. On the 26th of June, they were able to restore to Byzantium, after its sixteen years of Turkish occupation, the town which had been the scene of one of the first solemn assemblies of Christendom, the Council of Nicaea, in 385.

This first exploit represented an enormous success, both material and moral. The Turks, masters of the Orient, who had made the Empire of Byzantium tremble, suddenly found themselves driven back by an expedition from afar, by strangers to their land. For the first time, they had the impression, to use the words of René Grousset "that a force superior to the Turkish force had arisen".

Indeed, in spite of the innumerable difficulties resulting from the climate, the merciless combats, and also from their own internal quarrels, the Crusaders were to force their way doggedly on to Jerusalem.

They left Nicaea at the end of June, 1097, to cross the high plateaux of Anatolia. On reaching Lefke, they divided into two groups to facilitate provisioning in the Phrygian Plains. From the material point of view, the separation had its advantages, but it also weakened the expedition. As early as the 1st of July, Bohemund and his Normans were suddenly attacked by the Turks on a level with Dorylaeum. The encounter might have turned to disaster for the Normans, who were taken by surprise and disconcerted by the Turkish archers who decimated their ranks. Bohemund had had the time, however, to send runners to warn the other groups, so that the Turks, just as they were beginning to feel sure of victory, found themselves encircled. The battle of Dorylaeum, coming immediately after the recapture of Nicaea, consolidated the feeling of moral superiority from which the Franks were to benefit.

Three days later, the knights went on again, through Phrygia. On this occasion, natural difficulties alone were to stand in their way, but these would have been enough to discourage more than one army. They had to cross a wild, arid, uninhabitable steppe in the middle of July with no other source of water than the swamps of the region. Their itinerary is roughly that of the present railway line of Anatolia between Polybotos and Philomelion. Only after a month did they reach a more fertile region beyond Laodicaea, the town of Iconium (present-day Konya). Much to their surprise, they found it empty, not only of inhabitants but also of supplies. After this halt, however, the Armenians, who were cruelly oppressed by the Turks and welcomed the Crusaders as their liberators, were to help them. On several occasions, this "fifth column" was to facilitate their task.

The desert between Iconium and Heraclea was crossed without over-great difficulty thanks to the water which the Crusaders carried in leathern bottles, as the Armenians had advised them to do. After a skirmish before Heraclea which finished in further defeat for the Turks, the army again divided into two sectors, Tancred and a small band of Normans making for Cilicia with Baldwin, Godfrey of Bouillon's brother, while the main body of the expedition headed northeast, around the Anti-Taurus, to get to Caesarea of Cappadocia by the Nigde road. Toward the 3rd of October, they arrived at Placentia where they were welcomed as saviors by the Armenian population. They went on from there to Goksun, another Armenian town, and then crossed the Anti-Taurus to Marash. On the 21st of October, their advance guard reached the iron bridge over the Orontes to the east of Antioch. The Crusaders caught their first glimpse of Syria here, the goal of the Crusade.

Their objective could be no other than Antioch. The town which had been the scene of St. Peter's first preachings was one of the great strongholds of the period. There were four hundred towers on the walls, making the city practically impregnable. The Turks had been able to capture it only through treachery. The siege was to last for seven months, from the 21st of October, 1097, to the 3rd of June, 1098. The Crusaders would probably not have succeeded without the arrival of thirteen Genoese ships at the port of St. Simeon, on the mouth of the Orontes, allowing them to communicate with the coast and receive supplies. A boat bridge was made over the river by the Franks, permitting them to go from one side to the other. A pirate, Guynemer of Boulogne, meanwhile captured the port of Laodicaea from the Turks. The conquest of the Syrian coast thus began by isolated blows.

THE SIEGE OF ANTIOCH was probably the most dramatic episode on the way to Jerusalem. In reality it took place in two distinct parts. First there were the seven months spent before the citadel, which they almost despaired of taking in spite of their war machines.

The Crusaders went as far as building a whole castle, called Malregard opposite one of the gates in the walls. Supplies were scarce in the region and the morale of the troops, whatever their rank, gradually declined.

Finally a second castle, the Château Raymond or Château de la Mahomerie was erected on the right bank of the Orontes, opposite the bridge, and a sortie of the besieged Turkish garrison met with disaster. The cunning Bohemund took an Armenian renegade into his service who promised to deliver one of the towers on the wall. Sixty Franks entered the latter in the night of the 2nd of June and, in the morning, the Norman chief was able to hoist his banner on one of the heights of the city. Panic spread through the town, fostered by the Christian part of the population (Syrians and Armenians), who, here again, welcomed the Crusaders as their deliverers. After a seven months' siege, the army of Godfrey entered the stronghold.

It was high time. The very next day, the 4th of June, a great army of reinforcements, commanded by the governor of Mosul, Kerbogha (the Corboran of the poem of Antioch), appeared within sight of the city. Twenty-four hours earlier, this would probably have brought disaster to the Crusade. But Kerbogha had been delayed on the way, before Edessa, which was then in the hands of Baldwin of Bouillon. The situation of the Crusaders was nonetheless extremely grave. Kerbogha encamped around Antioch and, after being the besiegers, the Crusaders now became the besieged. The town was without supplies and a terrible famine began to be felt. To make the situation even worse, a few of the Crusaders fled and reached the port of St. Simeon, and from there the stronghold of Philomelion, in Asia Minor, where the emperor Alexis, at the head of a large Byzantine army, was preparing to come to the aid of Antioch. Out of panic or cowardice, the fleeing Crusaders spread the rumor that the Crusade was lost and that the Frankish army was destroyed. Judging that the game was up, Alexis turned round, leaving the defenders of Antioch to their fate.

"Whosoever found a dead cat or dog ate it with much relish", writes one chronicler. Further defections were to be feared from this decimated army, already worn out by its previous great efforts and exhausted with hunger. It was Bohemund of Tarente who saved the morale of the troops on this occasion, forcing the defenders to take their places on the walls. He even went as far as setting fire to the town one evening to compel the knights to go on the walls. Yet, at this time when they had just learnt of the departure of Alexis Comnenus, and despaired of all material aid, it was finally a purely spiritual event which changed the face of things. On the 14th of June, a priest from Provence, Peter Barthélémy, discovered the holy lance with which the soldier had pierced the side of Christ at Golgotha. He had seen it in a dream, in the foundations of the church of St. Peter of

Antioch, hidden under the paving slabs, and his revelations were found to be exact. The discovery raised the spirits of the Crusaders. On the 28th of June, in the morning, they made a sortie from the gate of the Château de la Mahomerie, and the chronicler writes:

> Our Lord sent them his grace which gave them such hardihood that those who the day before were lazy and thin and could not hold themselves up for weakness became strong and free so that their arms weighed on them as nothing.

The fact is that after several attacks the Turkish army dispersed and Kerbogha fled, pursued as far as the Iron Bridge. He left behind enormous plunder, including abundant victuals, and one can imagine the joyous feasting of the Crusaders on the evening of this great day.

The brusque return of plenty proved to be nearly as disastrous to the Crusade as the previous famine and defeat. In council a few days after this brilliant 28th of June, 1098, the barons decided to allow their exhausted troops to recover a little before marching on to Jerusalem and, remembering the terrible suffering endured on the Anatolian Plateau, to spend the summer at Antioch before starting out again in the following November. This may have been wise, but one cannot help wondering if it would not have been more prudent to take advantage of the shock they had given the Moslem world by defeating Kerbogha and to go on without delay. On the other hand, an epidemic broke out in the army, carrying off an important victim in the person of Adhemar of Monteil. Through his position and personality, he alone would have been capable of preventing the Frankish forces from dispersing and of assuring their unity.

The following six months were spent in prolonged inactivity interrupted only by small expeditions to the neighboring towns, such as Albara, to the east of the Orontes, or Marra (Ma'arat al Numan). But above all, the chiefs of the army wasted their time in disputes over the cities of Antioch or Marra. They seem completely to have forgotten that the initial aim of the Crusade was Jerusalem. Only the common folk and humble soldiers remembered. One fine day, their indignation reached its pitch: "Quarrels over Antioch. Quarrels over Marra. Every time God delivers a stronghold into our hands, our princes begin to dispute." And to remove the object of the issue, they began to demolish the walls of Marra.

The effect produced by such a revolt shows how great repentance can be in true believers, however carried away they may have been by their passions. A few days later, a strange pilgrim crossed the gates of Marra barefoot and set off southwards, in the direction of Jerusalem. It was Raymund of Saint Gilles, whose gesture shows that he had not forgotten his vow. His troops followed. After fifteen months in northern Syria, the Crusade had started out again. The first halt was at Capharda, and then Shaizar on the Orontes. The emir of Shaizar, frightened at the coming of the Crusaders, supplied them with guides and promised them safe-conduct through the valley of the Sarut. From there, after some hesitation as to whether it were better to go on to the coast or to march straight on to Jerusalem, the latter plan was adopted. The Crusaders passed through Masyaf, Raphanaea and the Boqa Plain. After a brief engagement, the Franks captured the latter and celebrated the feast of the Purification (2nd of February) in the Castle of the Kurds (Qal'at al Hosn). They went on from there to the little fortified town of Arqa, north of Tripoli, where they were to stay for some time, laying siege, to a number of important surrounding strongholds, such as the fortified port of Tortosa which was useful for supplies. English squadrons entrenched at Laodicaea brought the wheat, meat and oats necessary for the men and beasts of burden regularly to Tortosa. An agreement was also concluded with the emir of Tripoli who supplied guides through the gorges along the Lebanese coast, enabling the Crusaders to reach Tyre and Acre. This passage was of decisive importance, for the knights would otherwise never have been able to reach these towns in safety by the narrow corridors of the coastal massif which were defended by several fortresses. On the evening of the 19th of May, they came in sight of Beirut.

The caliph of Cairo, on whose territory the Crusaders now were, attempted at this point to persuade the knights to abandon their march. The safety of pilgrims to Jerusalem would be guaranteed. But the Christians had not come all this way and endured such hardship for a few vague promises, the worth of which history had already shown. They replied that, with the aid of God, they would complete the pilgrimage "all together, shoulder to shoulder in battle, and lances high." On the morrow, they went on their way again, through Sidon, Sarepta, Tyre and Acre. They celebrated Whitsun (the 29th of May) at Caesarea, before going on to Ramle, where they camped, and then Emmaus (El Qubeiba). Here the Christians of Bethlehem, Greeks and Syrians as well as members of the Latin Church, came to meet them, receiving with great joy the news of their forthcoming delivery. At last, on the 7th of June, 1099, the Frankish army came within sight of the walls of Jerusalem.

> When they heard Jerusalem named, then began they to weep and went down on their knees and gave thanks to Our Lord with many great sighs in that He had so loved them that they would see the end of their pilgrimage, the Holy City that Our Lord had so loved He had chosen here to save the world. Great pity was it to see and hear the tears and cries of these noble men... They raised their hands to heaven; then all, removing their shoes, kissed the ground. Whosoever saw this sight could not but be moved.

The Crusaders had reached the end of their pilgrimage, but were yet far from the end of their pains. Jerusalem was well fortified and the city was prepared for war. All the wells around the town had been dried up and the springs poisoned. Instructed by experience, the governor had turned out the local Christians. It was the month of June and the beginning of the hot period. Water holes were few and far between and supplies grew short. A first attack on the 13th of June failed, the war machines of the Crusaders proving insufficient. Dangerous long-distance expeditions to fetch wood for new siege engines now had to be made. Nonetheless the Crusaders had regained their old spirit. On the 8th of July, after a day's fasting, they went in solemn procession round the walls of Jerusalem as far as the Mount of Olives. The Moslems on the towers along the walls shouted insults and erected crosses to spit on them, committing all kinds of outrages to exasperate the knights. It was with fresh ardor that, on the morrow, the Crusaders wheeled one wooden tower into position on Mount Sion, a second beside the Kidron, and a third on the west corner of the walls. Godfrey of Bouillon and his brother Eustace of Boulogne, wearing freshly killed animal hides to protect themselves from the flaming projectiles known as "Greek fire", then stormed the walls and entered the El Aksa Mosque in the Temple enclosure. The whole of the army followed and by Friday, the 15th of July, 1099, the heart of the Holy City was in the hands of the Christians. The massacre which followed is, in truth, a "stain in the story of the Crusades," as William of Tyre said as early as the 12th century, but it may be accounted for, if not excused, by the suffering the knights from Europe had endured to reach their goal and, still further, by the sacrileges and provocations they had witnessed during the siege of the Holy City.

THE WAY WHICH THE FIRST CRUSADERS had forced through to Jerusalem again was to remain open for two centuries. Throughout this period, which coincided with the most brilliant epoch of the feudal age, the Holy Land and its approaches remained the bastion of Christendom, with its castles and ramparts, the mighty ruins of which still defy the imagination today. A whole chain of fortified towns stretched along the coast from Antioch to Ascalon, the "Virgin of Syria," the impregnable stronghold which the knights nonetheless captured in 1153—Tortosa, Tripoli, Sidon, Tyre, Acre and Jaffa. Inland, some guarding the plains while others commanded the mountain passes, stood Chastel Blanc, Blanche Garde, Beaufort, Beauvoir, Chastel Pélerin, Pierre du Désert and, the most imposing of all, the Krak des Chevaliers, their fine old names bringing a touch of Medieval poetry to the land of the Bible.

But the Crusaders were not only builders of castles. On their arrival in Cilicia, they had begun a basilica to St. Paul which may be the oldest religious construction of the Crusaders in the Holy Land. Hugh of Vermandois, the brother of the French king, was buried there in 1102, soon after the creation of the Latin kingdom. This first edifice was to be followed by a large number of new buildings and restorations. Only ten days after the fall of Jerusalem, Godfrey of Bouillon had founded a religious order with a chapter of twenty canons who were assigned to watch and pray at the tomb of Christ. This community was the origin of the regular canons of the Holy Sepulchre, who wore a white mantel bearing a red cross with double bar, later the vestment of the knights of the Holy Sepulchre. They rebuilt the ancient basilica founded by St. Helena after the discovery of the Cross, and on the 15th of July, 1149, a new church of the Holy Sepulchre was dedicated. Built to serve as a choir to the *Anastasis*, it included the rotunda marking the site of the tomb of Christ, which had been rebuilt in 1048. A whole ensemble of conventual buildings was erected, as in St. Jerome's time, with a cloister, dormitories, and refectory for the use of the chapter. Not far from this monastery stood a Benedictine abbey, founded in 1063 by merchants of Amalfi to provide a hostel for pilgrims from Europe, that was to become famous: the Hospital of St. John. One of the Crusaders from Provence, Gérard, together with a few other knights, took over its direction and the order of the Knights Hospitallers, who wore a black mantle with a white cross, thus came into existence. All the while remaining faithful to its original charitable end, the community of the Knights Hospitallers was soon to become a semi-military order.

Such a change is most understandable, considering that, once the vow of the Crusade was accomplished and Jerusalem delivered, only about three hundred knights and not many more foot soldiers remained in the Holy Land. The positions gained by the Crusaders were difficult to defend with so few men and the hope of reinforcements was extremely small, as soldiers could not be maintained in arms above the normal period of service, which was forty days in the Middle Ages. The only practical solution was the creation of a permanent militia of knight monks and, in 1118, Hugh of Payens and seven other French knights assumed the task of guarding the road from the coast to Jerusalem. King Baldwin gave them lodging in his former palace, on the esplanade where the El Aksa Mosque stood, while the Mosque of Omar, or cupola on the rock, the former Temple of Solomon, became their church. From the latter comes the name of Templars, as these knights who wore a white cloak with a simple red cross came to be called. The order was to grow so powerful that there were no less than nine thousand commanderies scattered throughout the East and the West at the time of their sudden arrest in France, heralding the suppression of the entire order.

It was these monk soldiers who shouldered the burden of defending the Holy Land

and it was they who built or restored the fortresses in which a whole army could take shelter along with the neighboring peasants. The Krak des Chevaliers held two thousand soldiers while, at Margat, four Hospitallers and twenty-eight men at arms mounted guard every evening. In an emergency, the walls of Margat could hold the local population of ten thousand. Saphed, which took the Templars only two and a half years to build, housed a garrison of seventeen hundred men in peacetime. It had wells and deep cisterns to ensure the water supply and huge caves in the rock were filled with victuals. The strongholds communicated with one another by means of beacons.

This great wave of building was not without consequences in Europe, where the Crusaders who had returned home began to erect edifices recalling the architecture of those of the Holy Places, often to house relics. Many are the rotundas which have been attributed without discrimination to the Templars. As to the relics brought back from the Near East, the most famous is that of the Crown of Thorns for which St. Louis built the Sainte-Chapelle in Paris.

With the Moslem population living in the Frankish states a *modus vivendi* was soon set up. "The Moslems are masters in their own homes and govern themselves as they please," notes an Arabian traveller, Ibn Jobait, little to be suspected from his other writings of sympathy for the Christians. Religious tolerance, in spite of all that may be said of the Middle Ages in this respect, seems to have been fairly well maintained. It is the same Moslem chronicler who writes:

> At Acre, though the former mosque has been turned into a Christian church, the Franks have left a corner to the Moslems, which is a veritable mosque within a church... Moslem and infidel are thus united in this mosque and each says his prayers facing the direction of his faith.

But the balance of power achieved by the Crusaders was twice to be shaken in the 12th century: a first time when Edessa was captured by the emir of Mosul and the whole of Europe sprang to attention at the great voice of St. Bernard ringing out from the hill of Vézelay, and a second time in 1187 when, after acting with the greatest rashness, the Frankish knights were annihilated by the armies of Saladin on Mount Hattin. This second occasion was by far the more serious; Jerusalem was to surrender to the conqueror, never to be recovered.

One would have thought that the Latin kingdoms, by now nearly one hundred years old, had gone for ever, though with an unbelievable return of energy they were actually to subsist for yet another century. They were reduced, of course, to a narrow coastal strip whose fortified towns had resisted, Tyre in particular.

The Frankish capital was no longer Jerusalem, but Acre. When the struggle became hopelessly unequal, between a Europe that seemed ever further away, absorbed in its own internal quarrels, and a strong and united Orient, it was at Acre that the final act of the Crusades in Syria was to unfold. During this last page of glory, Hospitallers and Templars, forgetting the quarrels which had divided them only too often, rivalled in valiance to such an extent that the Mamelukes were obliged three times to lay siege to the stronghold. In their fury, they slaughtered the entire population and destroyed the splendid walls along which two chariots could run side by side. The cathedral was razed to the ground and the door carried off to Cairo, where it may still be seen.

As soon as the Syrian coast had fallen into the hands of the Crusaders, the sea route had become much more popular than the overland route. The last Crusade of any importance to have come entirely overland was that of Frederick Barbarossa, which was, moreover, remarkably well organized. The German Emperor made his way through Gallipoli, the Byzantine provinces of Lydia and Phrygia and, in spite of the hostility of the Byzantines, was able to cross the deserted plateaux of Anatolia without too heavy losses, owing to his extremely strict discipline. In 1190, he arrived at Konya (Iconium), which he took by storm and, after securing supplies, went on through Laranda across eastern Isauria to the port of Seleucia. His army, almost entirely intact, was on the march towards Tarsus and Antioch, striking terror into the whole of the Moslem world including Saladin himself, when Frederick was drowned in the Selef. The most pitiful rout now took place. "These Germans, formerly so dreaded," writes an Arabian historian, "fell so low that they were sold off cheaply on the markets." The splendid army of Barbarossa, the value of which depended entirely on the presence of its leader, disappeared overnight.

Shortly after Barbarossa, the kings of England and France took the cross at Vézelay. Richard Cœur de Lion sailed from Marseilles and Philippe Auguste from Genoa. They had decided to put a truce to their quarrels to go to the aid of the Holy Land then in such sore distress, but they still deeply mistrusted one another and this caused many disagreements, preventing their Crusade from giving any real result. The two sovereigns joined forces at Messina where, for no apparent reason, they stayed for six months. Philippe Auguste was the first to leave (30th of March, 1191) for Acre, where he arrived after twenty days' crossing. The siege of the town recaptured by Saladin had started at the end of August, 1189. The Franks were to take the stronghold the following July. Meanwhile, the king of England had been thrown by a storm onto the coast of Cyprus and, having been received with hostility by the Byzantines, resolved in a moment of ill-humor to conquer the island. He landed at Limassol, occupied Larnaka, and besieged Famagusta and finally Nicosia, the capital. This unexpected episode was to be of great help to the Crusaders in later years, for Cyprus, with its harbors and rich farms was to allow the soldiers on the Syrian coast to be supplied with fresh vegetables. Cyprus, like Rhodes, was also to become the seat of a brilliant Franco-Greek civilization, traces of which are still to be seen today.

After the recapture of Acre and the coastal towns, communications between the ports of the western Mediterranean and the Syrian coast increased. It has even been said that, while Frankish Syria was created by faith, "it owed its survival in the 13th century to the spice trade." It is indeed true that to European merchants, especially the Italians, these overseas posts were an excellent opportunity for enrichment. A huge international trade circuit thus grew up which for a hundred years and more was to bring extraordinary prosperity to the towns of Italy and helped maintain western power in Syria, though it also brought the rivalries and sordid struggles born of trade. Many times the latter paralyzed the efforts of the Crusaders, giving the Moslems the shameful spectacle of Christians divided against themselves. At Acre, a street war between Genoese and Venetian merchants—it has come to be known as the war of St. Sabas—dragged on for two years (1256-1258).

A stop was now made regularly on the sea route at Cyprus. Frederick II, emperor of Germany, even tried to capture the island. He was a singular figure for a Crusader—excommunicated, he was hostile to the Franks and favored Islam, declaring that he had come to the East to hear the cry of the muezzin from the top of the mosque towers. The emperor's expedition was, however, entirely fruitless.

A LITTLE LATER, a Crusader of quite another kind was to set out on the same route: St. Louis, the story of whose voyage has come down to us through the chronicles of Joinville. These form one of the most complete narratives we possess of these overseas campaigns.

The first consequence of St. Louis' Crusade was the construction of a port and even a whole town. The Capetian kings had access to the sea through the delta of the Rhône, but no proper harbor. Marseilles and Montpellier were then part of the Holy Roman Empire. St. Louis, whose expedition was masterfully organized, did not hesitate to construct a port for the needs of the Crusade and Aigues-Mortes was thus created. The walls, which date from a little after the actual foundation of the town (1244), give us a very good idea of what the defences of a 13th-century stronghol were like. It is from here that the king sailed, on the 25th of August, 1248. The knights who followed the king, all French, hired ships from the neighboring ports, mainly Genoa and Marseilles.

St. Louis had orered provisions to be stored in readiness for him at Cyprus two years in advance and the king was welcomed on the island with great rejoicing. In the spring of 1249, he left the port of Limassol, where the fleet had assembled and, as Joinville writes:

> It was a most fine thing to see, for it seemed that all the sea, as far as the eye could reach, was covered with the sails of ships, which were numbered at eighteen hundred vessels, as many great as small.

The king sped across the Mediterranean on his ship, the *Montjoie*, towards the coast of Egypt, where he was to arrive on Friday, the 4th of June, in view of the Nile delta, before the city of Damietta. The Crusaders had already captured the latter after a lengthy siege (eighteen months), only to lose it again later within a period hardly longer than the siege itself. It was there that the Crusaders of St. Louis landed, under the eyes of the Mameluke horsemen armed from head to foot. Joinville's narrative gives a vivid picture of the mixture of almost garish grandeur and tranquil courage which characterizes the feats of arms of this period. One has the impression that the colors, the forms, the blare of the trumpets, and the brilliantly colored coats of arms are as much part of the battle as the blows and exploits themselves.

> It was he who arrived most splendidly, *writes Joinville, speaking of John of Ibelin, Lord of Jaffa, one of the most valorous Crusaders of all times,* for his galley was all painted within and without with the escutcheon of his arms which are of gold with a cross of gules. He had a fair three hundred oarsmen in his galley and each of them carried a buckler bearing his arms and every buckler bore an escutcheon of beaten gold. As he came into harbor, it seemed that the galley flew as the rowers strained on the oars, and that the thunder fell from heaven with the noise of the |bucklers, and the drums and the kettledrums and the Saracen horns, which were in his galley. As soon as the galley was beached as high as could be, he and his knights jumped down from the galley, well armed and finely attired and came to stand by us.

It should not be forgotten that this splendid scene took place under the gaze of the Turks on the shore, whose cavalry was to be put to flight by these ardent Franks who had just landed. Damietta fell unaccountably at a single blow.

The king's brother, Robert of Artois, the "evil genius" of the Crusade, was to compromise by his rashness the success to be expected after this brilliant opening feat of arms, but the four years which the king spent in the Holy Land, rebuilding the fortifications and restoring peace and justice, nonetheless permitted the Latin kingdoms to survive for fifty years longer. Biographers describe St. Louis carrying a mason's hod on the walls of Caesarea which he helped restore. At Jaffa, Sidon and Acre, too, there are traces of his work. While Romanesque architecture had been at the height of its development when the churches of Nazareth,

St. Anne of Jerusalem, Beirut and Sebastis had been built, Gothic now made its appearance with the cathedral of Our Lady of Tortosa, the church of Athlit and, above all, the admirable edifices in Cyprus, at Nicosia and Famagusta.

THE CHRONICLE OF MOREA, which Brother Juan Fernandez of Heredia, grand master of the Hospital of Rhodes, ordered to be written in the 14th century, begins like a medieval epic:

> At the time when the emperor Baldwin took Constantinople, a knight called William of Champlitte, brother of the Count of Champagne, having learnt of the great conquests which Baldwin, Count of Flanders, had made, decided to make his way to the Orient with men at arms to conquer lands as Baldwin, Count of Flanders, had done.
> With the aid of his brother, and the king of France, and with the money he obtained by mortgaging his lands, he assembled a great company of men at arms, barons and knights of Champagne, Burgundy, Germany, Normandy, Brittany and Picardy and, in the year one thousand two hundred and five after the birth of Our Lord, the said Lord William of Champlitte started out with all his men and arrived in Morea at a town in ruins which was formerly known as Achaie.
> There, seeing that the land was good, he descended from his horse with all his men; and they made an earthen wall where the town had formerly stood and there rested for a few days to take counsel as to the lands they wished to conquer.

During the first years of the 13th century, indeed, a curious change had come over both the spirit and the itinerary of the Crusades. The knights—including Geoffrey of Villehardouin, the Seneschal of Champagne, who was later to be their chronicler—had allowed the Venetians to persuade them to conquer Constantinople. More than once, it is true, the Byzantines had tried to hinder rather than help the Crusaders, but such a conflict was nonetheless, to use the words of Pope Innocent III, an "ungodly war" setting Christians against Christians, scattering their forces, awakening the thirst of conquest and weakening the Frankish colony just when the existence of the Holy Land was at stake.

The tourist of the 20th century may, however, attempt to pardon, if not approve, this untimely thirst for conquest which has left such magnificent vestiges. For, here again, as elsewhere, the Frankish barons constructed infinitely more than they destroyed, and it is perhaps in this strange Romano-Byzantine kingdom, stretching from the shores of the Bosporus to the Peloponnese, that the most handsome remains of their industry are to be found and, in the case of Rhodes, the most complete examples of their work.

Robert of Clari's narrative of the double siege of Constantinople is a veritable commentary in modern newspaper style. (The author, a "poor knight" of Picardy, whose estates covered an area of no more than fifteen acres, endowed his native parish of Corbie with rich treasures from the palace of Boucoleon, of which a crystal reliquary cross is still in existence today). The same chronicler has left an account of the coronation of Baldwin of Flanders, which amazed the whole of Europe, accustomed to regarding the potentate of Byzantium as the greatest temporal power and, indeed, the only power going back to ancient times. A mere count of Flanders had achieved, without realising it, what had been an impossible dream to Barbarossa and Richard Cœur de Lion.

This historic day (16th of May, 1204) finished, like all coronations at Byzantium, with an immense banquet and races at the hippodrome. The new emperor assumed all the customs of his predecessors, including that of affixing a golden seal to all important documents instead of the ordinary waxen seal used by kings, barons and private individuals alike. In the medieval world, three powers alone shared the privilege: the emperors of the Holy Roman Empire, the emperors of Byzantium, and the city of Venice.

The latter, responsible for diverting the Crusade from its true end, and principal beneficiary from the change, did not neglect to take a large share of the spoils. To this day, the famous horses on the façade of St. Mark's are a strange witness to the transience of empires. These noble bronze beasts originally came from Alexandria, whence they were removed to Rome by Augustus. Three centuries later, Constantine carried them off to Byzantium, where they decorated the imperial box at the hippodrome. It was from there that they emigrated to Venice at the beginning of the 13th century. Their adventures had not ceased, however, for after his Italian campaign, Napoleon took them to Paris to decorate the Carrousel Arch. They were returned to Venice in 1815, where they are still—for how long, none can say.

The Frankish barons seem to have found a second homeland in Greece, where, after a few initial skirmishes, they settled down peacefully. Their most recent historian, Jean Longnon, whose excellent pages are easier to read than a novel, relates how, with their feudal way of life and thought, they were closer to the spirit not of classical Greece, but of the Homeric Greece of large estates on which princes and shepherds lived simply from the fruits of the earth, and were always willing to stop and listen to bards or jongleurs. The knights of Champagne or Picardy instinctively took the titles of Homer's heroes: Prince of Achaie, Lord of Thebes.

NEVER DID INVADERS ADAPT THEMSELVES so easily as did the Franks to this gracious and welcoming land. Greece was later to experience the most ferocious conquerors, from the Catalans to the Mameluke Turks, but the Frankish knights left only pleasant memories. The first of the settlers did, at least; towards the end of the 13th century, a second wave of invaders, lead by the ambitious Charles of Anjou, treated the population with much less comprehension and exploited the land. But in the time of the Champlittes and the Villehardouins, a real affinity grew up between Franks and Moreots. The knights left their lands to the peasants, their riches to the churches and Orthodox monasteries, and learned the language of the country. In a short time, "a most brilliant school of chivalry," to use the expression of Jean Longnon, was to blossom on the shores of Greece. This was something new to the inhabitants of Morea. Their land had been considered only as a dreary province by the former Byzantine officials and the great landed aristocracy would never have dreamed of dwelling elsewhere than at Constantinople. The forsaken cities, not the least of which was Athens, the melancholy capital, were now to be restored to life and activity, while the peasants grew prosperous and a great literary and artistic movement took place at the court of Morea, "more magnificent," say the chroniclers "than that of a great king."

The very names testify to this understanding between Franks and Greeks. Those of the towns were transposed into delightful medieval forms, Athens becoming *Satine,* Thebes, *Estive,* Klarentaza, *Clarence,* and Monemvasia, *Malvoisie,* while the Frankish knights who married Greek women hellenized their titles, Goeffrey of Triel changing his name to Geoffrey of Carytaena, John of Nully to John of Passava, and the Saint Omer family to that of Santammeri. This civilization was to reach its height in the reign of the Franco-Greek prince, William of Villehardouin, who was born at the castle of Calamata, married a princess of Epirus, spoke Greek as well as French, and wrote poetry in both the Homeric and medieval minstrel traditions. When he died in 1278, he was mourned by Greeks and Franks alike. This knight, who incarnated all the qualities of the perfect knight, was centuries later to attract the attention of Goethe, who portrayed him as the perfect hero in his second *Faust.*

Churches and castles soon rose all over the duchy of Athens and the principality of Morea, embellishing the towns and fortifying the roads. Their ruins are still a most moving sight. While little is left of the Gothic churches of Andreville (Andravida) - St. Sophia's built by the Dominicans, St. Stephen's which belonged to the Franciscans, St. James to the Templars, and St. Nicholas to the Carmelites—at least in Athens itself the little Gothic church of Hypandi is still standing. The delightful cloister of Daphni, where the dukes of Athens were buried, was built by the Cistercians of Our Lady of Bellevaux, and is very similar to that of Pontigny in France, while the church of Negrepont (Chalcis), with its flattened apse, recalls the churches of Champagne.

Above Andravida stands what is still the finest castle in Greece, Klemutsi, with its walls and keep. Smaller than the fortresses of Syria, those of Greece are often on the sites of former acropoles, like the Acrocorinth. In other cases, as at Mistra, crowning so extraordinarily the Byzantine town, they are new constructions. The castle of Cadmea at Thebes was originally decorated with paintings—already of a historical character, they showed the Crusaders' conquest of Syria—but unfortunately these were destroyed by the Catalans in the 14th century. The ancient foundations of Pylos, at Navarino, and those of Egosthens in the Gulf of Corinth in their turn received new walls and defences. In the northwest, the passages of the Aelide were guarded by the castles of Carytaena, Crèveccœur, St. Helena, Bucelet and St. George. The fortress of Quelmo commanded the valley of the Eurotas and that of Beauvoir the road from Corinth to Calamata. Yet others were built at Solone, Bodonitsa, Passava and Yeraki. Further north, between Constantinople and Salonika, the road was made safe over a distance of nearly four hundred miles—roughly twelve days' journey on horseback.

These fortresses, the remains of which still stand proudly in the sunshine of Greece, were very dear to the hearts of the barons. When the Latin Empire of Constantinople fell and Michel Palaeologus reconquered the capital in 1261 from the weak Baldwin II (who went as far as pawning to Venetian merchants the Holy Crown of Thorns which was redeemed by St. Louis,) he ordered William of Villehardouin to give up the four great castles of Laconia: Yeraki, Monemvasia, Mistra and Grand-Magne. William, taken prisoner at Castoria, together with the Greek despot of Epirus, his father-in-law, finished by yielding, though not without regret. He attempted to go back on this decision made in a moment of discouragement by invoking the feudal custom forbidding the surrender of fortresses without the consent of the barons. Being at Constantinople at the time, he sent one of his fellow prisoners to the duke of Athens. The latter, Guy de la Roche, made haste to summon together all the vassals and the subvassals. Most of the more high-ranking nobles had been taken prisoner at Castoria and so, after the feudal custom, it was their wives who attended the council. The assembly took place at Nikli (Tegea). Guy de la Roche asserted that the surrender of the fortresses would leave the way open to the enemy. But the ladies made a sentimental reply to the warrior's sound reasoning.

> Hearing this, the princess and the wives of the barons whose husbands were in prison, began to cry out, saying they wanted their husbands and that they were pleased to allow the said castles to be delivered into the hands of the emperor.

They recovered their husbands, but William of Villehardouin never recovered from the loss of his castles, and it was in an attempt to regain them that he made an alliance with the ambitious Charles of Anjou which finally rendered Morea a mere dependency of the Angevin kingdom of Naples and Sicily. The duchy of Athens was to remain independent until 1311, when the "flower of the Franco-Greek chivalry" was savagely exterminated on the shores of Lake Copais by Catalan mercenaries. A century later, the Turkish invasion wiped out the last vestiges of the Frankish civilization in Greece and the last duke of Athens, a Florentine, was strangled by order of Sultan Mahomet, three years after the fall of Constantinople.

THE TOURIST TO RHODES cannot help trying to imagine the famous "Colossus of Rhodes" which was one of the seven wonders of the world in its day. One may doubt if it would add much to the admirable harbor today, however. With its height of one hundred and five feet, the monument would probably be no more striking than the Statue of Liberty before New York, and rather disappointing to contemporaries of the Empire State Building. Even amateurs of statistics could not be kept amused for long by the caravan of nine hundred camels hired by the demolition contractor, a Jew of Emesa, to clear the harbor of debris after a second and last earthquake had struck the giant down.

The two thousand statues, of colossal size for the most part, which still decorated the city when Pliny described it in the 1st century A.D., are hardly to be regretted more.

This island devoted to the colossal, which still contains some of the most impressive vestiges of the Mycenian civilization, one day welcomed to its shores, however, those who may perhaps be called the true "Colossi" of Rhodes. Of flesh and blood, they were to build an art, not of estheticians, but of walls, fortresses churches and hospitals which, in spite of the gigantic struggles they have withstood, are still the splendor and the unrivalled attraction of Rhodes. The knights of the Hospital of St. John, the grand masters of which bore names curiously familiar to us through books on the history of art or literature—Aubusson, Heredia, Villiers de l'Isle Adam—constructed a heroic city which remains the most impressive and best preserved of medieval strongholds, after being the last bastion of resistance to the Turkish invasion in the eastern Mediterranean.

For centuries, Rhodes held out against the Turks. The same Sultan Mahomet II who made himself master of Constantinople and entered the ancient basilica of St. Sophia in triumph failed a few years later to capture Rhodes. Fifty thousand men, a hundred vessels, and a four-months siege did not succeed in breaking down the heroism of the knights nor the courage of the Greek population, to whom Rhodes was the last outpost before the Moslem world. Completely isolated, Rhodes was finally to succumb only in 1522, having survived Constantinople by three quarters of a century. Soliman the Magnificent in person directed the operations of the siege, which lasted for more than five months, and, deeply impressed by the valor of the one hundred and eighty surviving knights, allowed them to leave the island with the honors of war. It is said that he owed his victory to the coral and sponge fishers of the neighboring island of Simi, who knotted the cables of the Turkish siege engines underwater.

Yet time itself has failed to efface the two centuries of heroism and fervor which marked Rhodes. Traces of the extraordinary international army of monk soldiers, nurses, and builders are still to be found in the "inns" or residences of the knights of each "tongue" or division of the order. That of France still bears an inscription in the name of the great prior Aimery of Amboise. Around the ramparts, the names of some of the towers recall how each of the tongues was responsible for the guard of a sector. Thus the tower of Spain belonged to the tongue of Aragon, the tower of Italy to the tongue of the same name, and the gate of Amboise to the tongue of France, while the churches of the city reflect every blend of European Gothic art—that of Catalogna in the cathedral of St. John and that of France in St. Catherine's church. The palace of the grand masters of the order still stand proud and erect, almost intact. The Hospital of the Knights has outlived wars and restorations and, although it is now a museum, still testifies to the order's original ideal. For the Knights of St. John of Jerusalem never forgot, throughout their eventful history, that their order had been founded to care for pilgrims and for the sick, whom they entertained "as the lords and masters of the house," to quote their rules. They had not been at Rhodes for four years when the chapter general began building a huge hospital where, besides the sick in residence there, fourteen poor people dined daily at the monks' table. One may wonder if the walls of the hospital do not still echo at night with the beautiful "prayer of the sick" repeated every evening after compline in the great hall:

> Our lords and masters the sick, pray for peace, that God may send his heavenly peace to earth;
> Our lords and masters the sick, pray for the fruits of the earth, that God may multiply the same in such a manner that He may be blessed and Christianity sustained by them;
>
> . . . .
>
> Pray for the pilgrims who fare by sea or over land, that God lead them forth and lead them in all safety of their bodies and souls.
>
> . . . .
>
> Our lords and masters the sick, pray for yourselves and for all the sick throughout the world; that Our lord give them such health as need their bodies and souls.
> Ours lords and masters the sick, pray for the souls of your fathers and mothers and of all Christian people departed this life in this century or another; that God give them *requiem sepiternam*. Amen.

Rhodes was the scene of the last episode of the Crusades in the Orient. With the capitulation of the island died the last echo of an epic which shook all Europe. Exactly three hundred years were to pass before Greece regained her independence when, in 1822, another hero came to die on her shores—Byron, whose monument is at Missolonghi.

The astonishing pageant of the Crusades has its light and its shade, its greatnesses and its weaknesses; such will ever be the case in the history of mankind. This short essay cannot attempt to decide in what measure, to use the term of the chroniclers, the straw is mixed with the good seed. The story is old enough for us, in the 20th century, to contemplate the great stone constructions along the roads of the Orient without drawing moral conclusions. Let us consider in silence only what the eye can see.

The ancient Egyptians left tombs, the Romans, triumphal arches, aqueducts and amphitheatres. In the steps of the Crusaders we find churches and fortresses, the traces of heroes and saints. It would be ridiculous to conclude that all were saints and heroes; yet such fortresses could never have defied the centuries with such serenity or the churches have retained such force of presence had there not been among them saints and heroes at least from time to time.

Régine Pernoud

I — SCEAU DE NOTRE-DAME DU PUY.

I — SEAL OF OUR LADY OF PUY.

2 — VÉZELAY: THE CROSS OF ST. BERNARD.

2 — VÉZELAY : LA CROIX DE SAINT BERNARD.

3 — BASILIQUE DE VÉZELAY : PORTAIL DU NARTHEX.

3 — BASILICA OF VÉZELAY: PORTAL OF THE NARTHEX.

4 — AIGUES-MORTES: TOWER OF CONSTANCE.

4 — AIGUES-MORTES : LA TOUR DE CONSTANCE.

PL. I — LA PRISE DE JÉRUSALEM.
(MINIATURE DU XIVᵉ S.)

PL. I — THE CAPTURE OF JERUSALEM.
(14TH CENTURY MINIATURE).

5 — REMPARTS DE CONSTANTINOPLE.

5 — THE WALLS OF CONSTANTINOPLE.

7 — MASSACRE DES CROISÉS
DE PIERRE L'HERMITE.
(ENLUMINURE DE 1490)

7 — MASSACRE OF THE FOLLOWERS
OF PETER THE HERMIT.
(ILLUMINATION OF 1490)

6 — SITE DE NICÉE.

6 — SITE OF NICAEA.

وكــاد ينزع الجمــال الشمر وانشـد

ما الحج سير ك نأوينا وادلاجا ولا الأغيام جمالا واحدلا أ

8 — 13TH CENTURY MOSLEM CARAVAN.
(ARABIAN MANUSCRIPT OF 1237 A.D.)

8 — CARAVANE MUSULMANE AU XIIIᵉ S.
(MANUSCRIT ARABE DE 1237 AP. J.-C.)

9 — JERUSALEM: THE CASTLE OF THE CRUSADERS.
→

9 — JÉRUSALEM : LE CHÂTEAU DES CROISÉS.
→

THE FRANKISH STATES
IN SYRIA

LES ÉTATS FRANCS
DE SYRIE

11 — GODEFROY DE BOUILLON TRAVERSE LE JOURDAIN.
(MINIATURE DU XIVᵉ S.)

10 — GISANT D'ÉLÉONORE D'AQUITAINE.
(ABBAYE DE FONTEVRAULT)

11 — GODFREY OF BOUILLON CROSSING THE JORDAN.
(14TH CENTURY MINIATURE)

10 — RECUMBENT FIGURE OF ELEANOR OF AQUITAINE.
(FONTEVRAULT ABBEY)

12 — CASTLE OF KERAK.

PL. II — THE KRAK DES CHEVALIERS.
→

12 — CHÂTEAU DE KÉRAK.

PL. II — KRAK DES CHEVALIERS.
→

13 — THE KRAK DES CHEVALIERS:
THE MILL TOWER.

→

13 — KRAK DES CHEVALIERS :
LA TOUR DU MOULIN.

→

14 — THE KRAK DES CHEVALIERS:
THE DOUBLE WALLS.

14 — KRAK DES CHEVALIERS :
LES DEUX ENCEINTES.

15 — KRAK DES CHEVALIERS :
PLACEMENT DE LA TABLE RONDE.

15 — THE KRAK DES CHEVALIERS:
SITE OF THE ROUND TABLE.

16, 17 AND 18 — THE KRAK DES
CHEVALIERS: ABOVE, MODEL
OF THE CASTLE; TO THE LEFT,
SITE OF THE OIL STORE;
TO THE RIGHT, CURB OF THE WELL.

16, 17 ET 18 — KRAK DES CHEVAL
EN HAUT, MAQUETTE DU CHÂTE.
A G., EMPLACEMENTS DES OUTRES A
A DR., LA MARGELLE DU PUIT

19 — THE KRAK DES CHEVALIERS: THE CHAPEL.

19 — KRAK DES CHEVALIERS : LA CHAPELLE.

20 AND 21 — ABOVE, LETTER FROM THE BISHOPS
OF THE HOLY LAND TO PHILIP AUGUSTUS;
TO THE LEFT, SEAL OF PHILIP AUGUSTUS.

20 ET 21 — CI-DESSUS, LETTRES DES ÉVÊQUES
ÉCRITES DE TERRE SAINTE A PHILIPPE-AUGUSTE ;
A G., SCEAU DE PHILIPPE-AUGUSTE.

22 AND 23 — ABOVE, SEAL OF RICHARD CŒUR DE LION; BELOW, SEAL OF FREDERICK BARBAROSSA.

PL. III — THE CAPTURE OF CONSTANTINOPLE. (14TH CENTURY MINIATURE)

→

22 ET 23 — EN HAUT, SCEAU DE RICHARD CŒUR DE LION; EN BAS, SCEAU DE FRÉDÉRIC BARBEROUSSE.

PL. III — LA PRISE DE CONSTANTINOPLE. (MINIATURE DU XVᵉ SIÈCLE)

→

24 — CONSTANTINOPLE: THE GREAT
DOOR OF ST. SOPHIA'S.

→

24 — CONSTANTINOPLE : LA GRANDE
PORTE DE SAINTE SOPHIE.

→

25, 26 AND 27 — ST. SOPHIA'S: TO THE LE[
THE VIRGIN AND CHILD (MOSAIC);
BELOW, TOMBSTONE OF THE DOGE,
ENRICO DANDOLO;
TO THE RIGHT, CHRIST OF MAJESTY (MOSAI[

25, 26 ET 27 — SAINTE-SOPHIE : A G., LA VIE[
ET L'ENFANT (MOSAÏQUE) : CI-DESSOUS, PIER[
TOMBALE DU DOGE HENRI DONDOLO ;
A DR., CHRIST EN MAJESTÉ. (MOSAÏQUE)

29 — ARMES DE VILLEHARDOUIN.
(PETITE MÉTROPOLE D'ATHÈNES)

29 — THE ARMS OF VILLEHARDOUIN.
(LESSER METROPOLITAN CHURCH OF ATHENS)

28 — SAINTE-SOPHIE : EMPLACEMENT
DU TRÔNE DE L'IMPÉRATRICE.

28 — BASILICA OF ST. SOPHIA: SITE
OF THE THRONE OF THE EMPRESS.

30 — ATHENS: THE LESSER METROPOLITAN CHURCH.

31 — MISTRA: REMAINS OF A STREET.
→

30 — ATHÈNES : LA PETITE MÉTROPOLE.

31 — MISTRA : VESTIGES D'UNE RUE.
→

32 — SITE OF MISTRA AND
THE METROPOLITAN CHURCH.

32 — SITE DE MISTRA ET
L'ÉGLISE DE LA MÉTROPOLE.

PL. IV — MISTRA : CHÂTEAU DE VILLEHARDOUIN.

PL. IV — MISTRA: VILLEHARDOUIN'S CASTLE.

33 — MISTRA: THE PALACE OF THE DESPOTS.
→

33 — MISTRA : LE PALAIS DES DESPOTES.
→

134 AND 35 — MISTRA: ABOVE,
THE CHURCH OF THE PANTANASSA;
TO THE RIGHT, THE MONASTERY OF BRONTOCHION.

34 ET 35 — MISTRA : CI-DESSUS,
L'ÉGLISE DE LA PANTANASSA;
A DR., LE MONASTÈRE DU BRONTOCHION.

36 — THESSALONIKA: THE WALLS.

36 — THESSALONIQUE : LES REMPARTS.

37 — THESSALONIQUE : ÉGLISE SAINT-GEORGES.

37 — THESSALONIKA: CHURCH OF ST. GEORGE.

38 — THESSALONIKA: THE CRYPT OF
THE BASILICA OF ST. DEMETRIUS.

39 — GULF OF NAUPLIA.
→

38 — THESSALONIQUE : LA CRYPTE DE
LA BASILIQUE SAINT-DÉMÈTRE.

39 — GOLFE DE NAUPLIE.
→

PL. V — VALLÉE DE L'ALPHÉE.

PL. V — VALLEY OF THE ALPHEUS.

42 — KLEMUTSI: THE CASTLE.

42 — KHLEMOUTSI : LE CHÂTEAU.

43 — KHLEMOUTSI : LA GRANDE
SALLE DU CHÂTEAU.

43 — KLEMUTSI: THE GREAT
HALL OF THE CASTLE.

44 — RHIUM.

44 — RION.

45 — LIVADIA.

46 — THE ACROCORINTH.

46 — L'ACROCORINTHE.

47 — REMPARTS DE L'ACROCORINTHE.

47 — WALLS OF THE ACROCORINTH.

DAT VACANCE P·O·E CANCELLARIA

48 — FOUNDATION LETTER OF THE
SAINTE-CHAPELLE BY ST. LOUIS.

48 — LETTRE DE FONDATION DE LA
SAINTE-CHAPELLE PAR SAINT LOUIS.

PL. VI — SAINT LOUIS PORTANT LES RELIQUES.
(VITRAIL DE LA SAINTE-CHAPELLE)

PL. VI — ST. LOUIS BEARING THE HOLY RELICS.
(WINDOW OF THE SAINTE-CHAPELLE, PARIS)

49 — MASSACRE OF THE FRANKS BY
TURKISH HORSEMEN AT MANSURA.
(15TH CENTURY MINIATURE)
→

49 — MASSACRE DES FRANCS PAR LES
CAVALIERS TURCS A LA MANSOURAH.
(MINIATURE DU XVe S.)
→

THE LAST
CRUSADE

LA DERNIÈRE
CROISADE

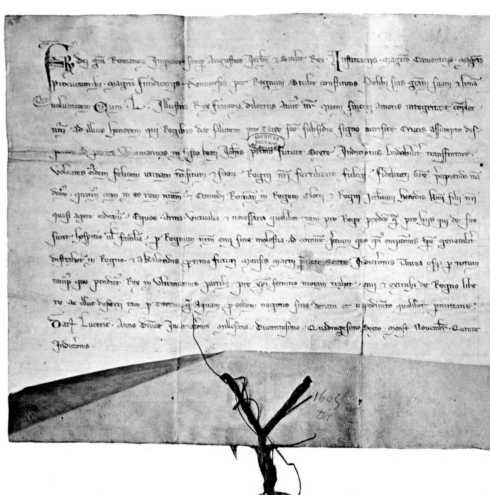

50 AND 51 — TO THE LEFT, STATUE OF ST. LOUIS (13TH CENTU[RY,]
CHURCH OF MAINNEVILLE); ABOVE, LETTER FROM THE EMPER[OR]
FREDERICK TO THE SICILIANS.

50 ET 51 — A G., STATUE DE SAINT LOUIS.
(XIIIᵉ S., ÉGLISE DE MAINNEVILLE) ; CI-DESSUS,
LETTRE DE L'EMPEREUR FRÉDÉRIC II AUX SICILIENS.

53 — THE DESERT OF NEGEV.

LE DERNIER BASTION
RHODES

THE LAST OUTPOST
RHODES

55 AND 56 — ABOVE, SEAL OF FULK OF VILLARET;
BELOW, SEAL OF VILLIERS DE L'ISLE ADAM.

54 — THE WALLS OF ACRE.

←

55 ET 56 — EN HAUT, SCEAU DE FOULQUES
DE VILLARET; EN BAS, SCEAU DE VILLIERS
DE L'ISLE-ADAM.

54 — LES REMPARTS DE SAINT-JEAN-D'ACRE.

←

57 — LINDOS: THE FORTRESS.

57 — LINDOS : LA FORTERESSE.

59 AND 60 — RHODES: ABOVE, THE FORMER INFIRMARY;
TO THE RIGHT, GATE OF KOSKINU.

59 ET 60 — RHODES : CI-DESSUS, L'ANCIENNE
INFIRMERIE; A DR., LA PORTE DE KOSKINOU.

61 — RHODES: HOUSE OF
THE CHAPLAINS OF FRANCE.

61 — RHODES : MAISON DES
CHAPELAINS DE FRANCE.

62 — RHODES : AUBERGE DE FRANCE
DANS LA RUE DES CHEVALIERS.

62 — RHODES: HOSTEL OF FRANCE,
ON THE RUE DES CHEVALIERS.

63 — RHODES: HOSTEL OF FRANCE.
(COAT OF ARMS)

63 — RHODES : AUBERGE DE FRANCE.
(LES ARMES)

64 — RHODES : COUR INTÉRIEURE DE
L'HÔPITAL DES CHEVALIERS.

64 — RHODES: INNER COURTYARD OF
THE KNIGHTS' HOSPITAL.

65 — RHODES: CHAPEL OF THE HOSPITAL.
(DETAIL)

65 — RHODES : CHAPELLE DE L'HÔPITAL.
(DÉTAIL)

PL. VIII — UNE COUR D'AUBERGE.　　　　　　　　　　　PL. VIII — A PILGRIMS' HOSTEL COURTYARD.

66 — RHODES: PALACE OF THE GRAND MASTERS

→

66 — RHODES : LE PALAIS DES GRANDS MAÎTRES.

→

67 ET 68 — RHODES, PALAIS DES GRANDS MAÎTRES :
A G., L'ENTRÉE; CI-DESSUS, LA COUR INTÉRIEURE.

67 AND 68 — RHODES: PALADE OF THE GRAND MASTERS:
TO THE LEFT, THE GATE; ABOVE, THE INNER COURTYARD.

69 — THE RETURN OF THE CRUSA[DE]
(CHAPEL OF THE GREYFRIARS MONAST[ERY]
AT NANCY, FRANCE)

69 — LE RETOUR DU CROISÉ. (CHAPE[L]
DU COUVENT DES CORDELIERS A NAN[CY]

HISTORICAL AND
ARCHAEOLOGICAL NOTES

PLATES IN BLACK AND WHITE

1. — *Seal of Our Lady of Puy.* It was in the magnificent cathedral of Puy, a great French pilgrim church dating from the 11th and 12th centuries, that the Crusade really began. In 1095, the bishop of Puy, Adhemar of Monteil, who had been a knight before becoming a priest, welcomed Urban II to this cathedral. The pope of the Crusade celebrated solemn mass here on the 15th of August, 1095, before going on to Clermont where the council at which it was decided to reconquer the Holy Places was held. Adhemar of Monteil, to whom the pope entrusted the spiritual leadership of the Crusade, set out with the main body of the expedition, but died on the threshold of the Holy Land, at Antioch, on the 1st of August, 1099. His episcopal ring was brought back to the cathedral and in his memory the canons of Puy claimed the right to wear armor during Eastertide. The sanctuary of Our Lady of Puy contained a highly venerated Black Virgin and was the most popular place of pilgrimage in France throughout the Middle Ages.

2. — *Vezelay: the Cross of St. Bernard.* This cross recalls the memory of the ardent advocate of the Second Crusade, St. Bernard, who preached at Vezelay on the 31st of March, 1146, before the circle of hills where all the greatest princes of Christendom had gathered. Louis VII of France took the cross here, together with a multitude of knights. The summons of the Abbot of Clairvaux was to reawaken the spirit which, fifty years earlier, had stirred the hearts of those who set out to defend the Cross against the Crescent. This second expedition unfortunately lacked military leaders of the same calibre as those of the First Crusade.

3. — *Basilica of Vezelay: Portal of the Narthex.* The portal of the narthex (one of the finest specimens of Romanesque sculpture in France; it dates from 1140-1150) bears a Pentecostal scene showing Christ sending out the Apostles to every part of the earth, including the Orient, the inhabitants of which were supposed at the period to have strange forms. (They were known, for instance, as the "long-eared people"). The signs of the Zodiac on the archivolt bear the same message: the universe is called to hear the words of Christ.

4. — *Aigues-Mortes.* Not the least consequence of the Crusades was the creation of the town of Aigues-Mortes. St. Louis (Louis IX of France) possessed no port on the Mediterranean, Marseilles and Montpellier, the two big ports in the south of France at the time being part of the Holy Roman Empire. The present walls of Aigues-Mortes (a perfect specimen of 13th-century constructions of this type) do not date from the actual lifetime of St. Louis. Only a small fortress, the *castrum*, was erected at the same period as the town, at the place where several arms of the Rhône meet in the pool of Psalmodi. This fortress, which is still standing and has remained unchanged from its original form, is the Tower of Constance. A massive

cylindrical building, it has a ground floor, upper stories, a gun platform on which stood a watch turret, and finally an iron framework which must have contained a beacon. The tower is some 100 feet high and stands in the middle of a wide moat.

5. — *The Walls of Constantinople*. It was under these walls, which four hundred years earlier had witnessed the failure of the Arab world's first attempt to overthrow Christendom (the Moslem siege of Constantinople, (717-718), that the three sections of the armies of the Crusaders, together with a band of Normans from Sicily, joined forces to march on the Holy Land. Here, too, the Crusaders met with their first disappointment, for the Emperor Alexis Comnenus, far from welcoming the knights from Europe as they had expected, desired only to obtain their promise to yield all future conquests to Byzantium. About a hundred years later, the same walls were to be stormed by the knights of the Fourth Crusade, whom the Venetians had cunningly persuaded to conquer Constantinople to satisfy their own commercial ambitions. The Crusaders' capture of Constantinople (9-12th of April, 1204) was also due to the long series of misunderstandings between the Franks and the Byzantines and to the mutual incomprehension which had largely contributed to the failure of previous Crusades.

6. — *Site of Nicaea*. It was at Nicaea that the Crusaders encountered the Moslems for the first time, the city being at the time the seat of the Seljuk kingdom of Anatolia. The stronghold was carried at a single stroke then by the fresh forces of the Crusaders and, in accordance with the agreements concluded with the emperor of Byzantium, was delivered into the hands of the latter (26th of June, 1097). Such a splendid feat of arms avenged the Turkish massacre of the Popular Crusade, which had met its fate on the coast of Bithynia one year earlier (21st of October, 1096).

7. — *Massacre of the Followers of Peter the Hermit*. This illumination of 1490 shows the last act of the Popular Crusade. The Turks bore down in fury upon the army of humble people won to the cause of the Holy Land by popular preachers, the most celebrated of whom, Peter the Hermit, was to become an almost legendary figure. The Popular Crusade had gone ahead of that of the knights and, without leaders or discipline, was to perish miserably beside the Gulf of Nicomedia (as depicted here ; in the background, are the walls and buildings of Constantinople).

The miniature belongs to a copy of the *Passages d'outremer* by Sebastien Marot, a canon of Troyes (France) and chaplain to Louis Laval, governor of the province of Champagne. The latter was offered the manuscript by his chaplain and appears to have been a discriminating bibliophile since he had his celebrated *Heures* illuminated by Jean Colomb. (Bibl. nat., Français 5594, fol. 21).

8. — *13th Century Moslem Caravan*. This Arabian manuscript of the *Seances de Hariri* gives some idea of the opulence of oriental trade at the time of the Crusades. Damascus was the great market for this type of caravan, which carried luxury products, spices and perfumes, later to supply the European merchants, mainly Italian and Provençal, who settled in Palestine. The caravan consists of both horses and camels ; one of the latter bears a closed palanquin containing the wife of the horseman to be seen on the left. This fine manuscript of the School of Baghdad attests a very sure decorative sense. It is dated 634 Hegira, 1237 A.D. (Bibl. nat., Fonds Arabe, 5847, fol. 94.)

9. — *Jerusalem: the Castle of the Crusaders*. Now the Greek monastery of the Holy Cross. The former castle, which still has a most martial air, lies in a vale planted with olive groves. The fine paved interior courtyard is lined with the monks' cells. According to legend, the tree out of which the Holy Cross was made grew in the centre of this monastery. A Georgian church was built over the place in the 11th century. The church contains 16th-century frescoes and a very interesting mosaic pavement showing curious legendary animals, which is itself a copy of tesserae dating from the 5th and 6th centuries. The tree of the Holy Cross was commonly acknowledged to have been planted by Lot as he fled from Sodom and Gomorrah. In medieval mysteries, the same tree is said to be that from which Eve ate the forbidden fruit, sharing it with Adam.

10. — *Recumbent Figure of Eleanor of Aquitaine*. This fine recumbent figure, together with that of Henry II Plantagenet (the second husband of Eleanor), both masterpieces of sculpture of the end of the 12th century, is in the Abbey of Fontevrault (France). Eleanor of Aquitaine, who had accompanied the king of France, her first husband, to the East, where she led a frivolous life, was repudiated by Louis VII after the Crusade. On her remarriage with Henry II, the great southern estates of her dowry became an English possession. The seal above the figure is that of Guy of Lusignan,

whose marriage with the heiress to the kingdom of Jerusalem was to produce a weak king, largely responsible for the disaster of Hattin in 1187. Guy de Lusignan later founded a dynasty at Cyprus (he acquired the island in 1192) which was originally captured from Isaac Comnenus by Richard Cœur de Lion.

11. — *Godfrey of Bouillon Crossing the Jordan*. This miniature is in two parts and is taken from the *Roman de Godefroy de Bouillon et de Saladin et de tous les autres rois qui ont été outre-mer jusqu'à Saint-Louis* (Narrative of Godfrey of Bouillon, Saladin and of all the other kings who ventured overseas up to the time of St. Louis ; 14th century manuscript). On the left, Godfrey of Bouillon and his companions are shown crossing the Jordan while, on the right, Godfrey is cutting off a camel's head at a single blow (the hero's strength was legendary). Godfrey is to be recognized from his arms which bear the five crosses of the kingdom of Jerusalem. The episode belongs to the struggles, dating from after the conquest of the Holy City, to reduce the coastal towns which were a perpetual menace to the Frankish kingdoms. The miniature is characteristic of those produced by Parisian artists at the beginning of the 14th century, who were all to a greater or lesser extent connected with the famous workshop of Honoré of the rue Boutebrie. The drawing is in fresh tints outlined in black, and the manuscript, which is dated 1337, contains 92 illuminated pages. (Bibl. nat., Français 22495, fol. 78.)

12. — *Castle of Kerak*. The castle of Kerak is the most remote and farthest south of all the strongholds forming the defence line of the Latin kingdom of the East. Saladin besieged the fortress in vain until 1187, when the disaster of Hattin was finally to allow the sultan to become the master of Palestine. The walls are 820 feet long and a moat some sixty feet wide originally separated the fortress from the nearby town. The halls containing the apartments of the commander opened onto small open-air courtyards and the castle also had underground halls lighted and aired by round openings to protect them from the excessive heat prevalent in the Dead Sea area. The east side of the fortress, with its four rectangular towers separated by curtain walls, has remained truer to its original appearance in the time of the Franks than other parts of the building. The keep, which is still standing, was built by the Arabs. It is of soft stone, unlike the extremely hard volcanic stone generally used by the Franks. A Romanesque chapel with cradle vaulting and a semicir-

cular apse has been found in the castle. Traces of painting were still visible on the chapel walls in the 19th century. Kerak with its castle is today one of the most important towns of Transjordan. The city walls still bear many vestiges of the work of the Crusaders.

13. — *Krak des Chevaliers: the Mill Tower*. The garrison of the Krak numbered up to two thousand soldiers, which means that the organization of supplies must have been a very serious matter. One 13th-century historian says that the castle had a store of victuals for five years in advance. Such reserves probably consisted mainly of cereals kept in the huge underground halls of the castle. The gun platform which held at least one windmill has also been discovered. That constructions of this type had mills is a well-known fact — there were twelve wind or water mills at the castle of Saphed, for instance, both in and outside the building. The castle's bread oven has likewise been discovered. This oven has a surface area of 226 square feet and must have had to be kept constantly fired, for even today, an oven of this size would need a month's continual heating before it could be used.

14. — *Krak des Chevaliers: the Double Walls*. The castle has double concentric walls forming a trapezium and defended by moats. From one end to the other, the first wall measures 720 feet and it is 440 feet at its widest part. On the west side, there are five handsome round towers, while the east side was fortified with rather less well finished salients. A crenelated sentry walk ran round the whole and brattices, both on the towers and the intermediary curtain walls, reinforced the position of the defenders in case of siege. The regular stone layers of this first wall probably mean that it was built in a single attempt. The second wall, which is separated from the first by moats and terrepleins, is also reinforced; there are four towers to the west and south. Inside the second wall were the living quarters, the chapel, and a huge hall nearly 400 feet long which formed the body of the original building. The superb gallery similar to a cloister which faces east and thus escapes the midday sun must have been a cool walk during the hottest hours of the day. The façade of the gallery opens on to the courtyard by two gates ans five bays resting on fine ogival colonettes which appear to have been executed in the middle of the 13th century. There is no keep proper, though a group of three towers joined together form the strongest part of the fortress. They stand on the weakest side, where the land itself offers no natural defence.

15. — *Krak des Chevaliers: Site of the Round Table.* This fine stone table stands inside the walls beside the chapel in the square courtyard.

16, 17 and 18. — *Krak des Chevaliers: Model of the Castle ; Site of the Oil Store ; Curb of the Well.* A very detailed model of the Krak des Chevaliers has been made from the drawings of Paul Deschamps and is now on display in the Museum of French Buildings (Musée des Monuments Français) at Paris. Our photograph was taken from the same angle as that of the Krak (see Pl. II).

The floors of the storerooms still show traces of the leathern bottles in which oil was kept. The water supply, which must have been considerable for such a large number of occupants, was ensured by cisterns. Nine of these have been found. They were fed by earthenware pipes carrying the rainwater down from the terraces. There was also a vast reservoir between the two walls. All the Syrian castles contained similar reservoirs which we would call swimming pools. The men bathed and the animals drank there. That of the Krak is 230 feet long and from 25 to 50 feet wide. It is of stonework throughout. Inside the castle itself, a well 90 feet deep has also been found. The curb of the latter bears traces of the ropes which were used to draw the water.

19. — *Krak des Chevaliers: the Chapel.* This is a 12th century Romanesque building and consists of a nave with three bays with pointed arches and a semicircular apse set in a square chevet which is part of the outside wall. It is somewhat similar in style to the Romanesque churches of Provence, especially that of Les Saintes Maries de la Mer. There are large bays to east and west and three rectangular windows. A porch with ribbed vaults opens onto the courtyard.

20. — *Letter from the Bishops of the Holy Land to Philippe Auguste.* This letter was composed by the bishops of Caesarea, Nazareth and Bethlehem, together with the abbots of the monasteries of Mount Sion, the Valley of Josaphat, Mount Tabor and the Mount of Olives, to describe to Philippe Auguste the wretched state of the Holy Land after the disaster of Hattin. Tyre and Acre alone remained in the hands of the Franks and even the area around the former were exposed to Saracen raids. The Arabs cut down the trees, uprooted the vines, burnt down the houses and destroyed all that came in their way, while the inhabitants were reduced to the greatest distress.

The letter, which is undated, is one of the appeals which resulted in the Third Crusade. The armies of Saladin had just recaptured Jerusalem and the very existence of the Latin kingdoms was at stake, though they were actually to subsist for more than a hundred years. (Musée de l'Histoire de France, A E III, 196.)

21, 22 and 23. — *Seal of Philippe Auguste ; Seal of Richard Cœur de Lion ; Golden Bull of Frederick Barbarossa.* Three illustrious Crusaders: the Emperor Frederick Barbarossa took the cross in 1189 and was to die in the Holy Land; Philippe Auguste and Richard Cœur de Lion captured Acre together in 1191.

24. — *Constantinople: the Great Door of St. Sophia's.* St. Sophia's has always been regarded as the foremost example of oriental Christian art. It was in 532 that Justinian decided to build the first basilica, on the site of a church dedicated to Holy Wisdom (*Haghia Sophia* — the origin of the name that was to be gradually altered to St. Sophia) two centuries earlier by Constantine. Its architects, Anthemius of Tralles and Isidorus of Miletus, completed it in less than five years and contemporaries say that the edifice was so light and aerial that it appeared "less to rest on stonework than to hang by a golden chain from heaven". It consisted of a huge dome 98 feet in diameter, the largest ever created, which rested on a drum held by two semivaults, one to the west and the other to the east, while two huge arches at the sides were themselves buttressed by the collaterals ; each of the two semicupolas was in its turn buttressed by three semicircular niches. The whole building thus supported the central dome, which was 180 feet above the ground. In 557, the edifice was shaken by an earthquake and the dome collapsed when the architect charged with restoring the basilica (the nephew of Isidorus of Miletus) erected scaffolding. The second dome was given a slightly more ovoid shape than the first to make it stronger. This new dome, completed in 562, can still be admired to day. The basilica of St. Sophia is gradually being restored to its original aspect.

The door still bears traces of the cross which was torn off by the Turks after the Conquest.

25, 26 and 27. — *St. Sophia ; Mosaics of the Virgin and Child ; the Tombstone of Enrico Dandolo ; Christ of Majesty.* The whole of the marvelous basilica of St. Sophia's was faced with mosaics. These mosaics, most of which were covered over after the Turkish conquest, when the church was turned into a mosque, are now gradually reappearing. The backgrounds are mainly of deep blue, set off by gold.

St. Sophia's contains the tombstone of Enrico Dandolo, the doge of Venice to whom the Crusaders at one time thought of giving the imperial crown after the capture of Constantinople in 1204. Dandolo refused however, and it was finally Baldwin Count of Flanders who was elected first Latin emperor of Constantinople.

This Christ of Majesty may be said to be characteristic of Byzantine art. This is an art based on the use of sumptuous materials and the process of the optical mixing of colors. The general shades are in many cases obtained by very varied tones, the combination of which has the appearance of a single color which gives at the same time a most vivid effect.

28. — *St. Sophia's: the Empress' throne.*

29. — *The Arms of Villehardouin.* These arms are carved on the pediment of the Lesser Metropolitan church at Athens, a delightful little Byzantine church which was for a short time the private cathedral of the bishops. Its walls are faced with marbles dating from both classical and Byzantine times. They include a frieze with the signs of the Zodiac from a monument going back to the 4th century B.C.

30. — *Athens: the Lesser Metropolitan Church.* This tiny church was the heart of medieval Athens, which was known to ancient chroniclers as Satine. The former cathedral dates from the beginning of the 13th century and is in the form of a Greek cross. It is now one of the most interesting curiosities of Byzantine Athens, together with the neighboring churches of Kapnikarea and the Sts. Theodores, which both go back to the 11th century.

31. — *Mistra.* The town of Mistra is the best-preserved Byzantine ensemble in Greece and gives an excellent idea of what a Gallo-Greek town was like in the time of the Villehardouins. Even its name was a Frankish gift, Mistra being a corruption of "mistress." The winding streets with a church or monastery at every turn have hardly changed since the 14th and 15th centuries. In the reign of the Palaeologi, it was the capital of Morea and a prosperous silk centre. The town was considered the pearl of the entire province. Captured by the Turks in 1460, and by the Venetians in the 17th century, Mistra finally fell into the hands of the Turks once more, and was gradually to decline while the present village grew up at its feet.

32. — *Site of Mistra and the Metropolitan Church.* Originally built to a basilical plan, the edifice was begun in 1310. Later, in the 15th century, a first floor was added in the form of a Greek cross, bringing about the defacement of the frescoes decorating the nave. The latter were restored to the light from their whitewash concealment at the end of the last century by Gabriel Millet, who the church into a kind of museum for the sculptures he found among the neighboring ruins. The church also contains a number of carved-marble doors, chancel plaques and iconostases, some of which go back to the 9th century. On one of the lintels are the arms of Isabella, the princess of Lusignan.

33. — *Mistra: the Despots' Palace.* The palace is a Composite building, containing traces of a number of different periods. A vaulted hall with pointed arch windows in the right wing dates from the 14th century, while the main part of the edifice consists of an immense vaulted hall with flamboyant Italianate windows going back to the 15th century. This palace, which the Turks named the Grand Bazaar, stands on the main square of the walled upper town of Mistra.

34 and 35. — *Mistra, the Church of the Pantanassa and the Monastery of Brontochion.* The Church is built to the same plan as the monastery, though the former has rather more elegant proportions and a bell tower which shows Gothic influence. It goes back to the first half of the 15th century and contains paintings dating from this period (including the famous portrait of Manuel Khatzikis in the narthex), together with many frescoes in the galleries (the Annunciation, the Presentation, the Transfiguration, etc.).

The former Monastery of Brontochion, which fell into ruins in the 19th century and was restored in 1939, was built at the beginning of the 14th century on Greek lines with five cupolas. Frescoes have recently been discovered here, notably that of the Adoration of the Virgin on the south side of the church, and several others in the central nave. (See SOTIRIOU, M. G., *Mistra* - Athènes, 1956.)

36. — *Thessalonika: the Walls.* These encircle the upper town of the famous city where Paul preached. (The saint seems to have had a particular affection for Thessalonika and, after spending the winter of 49-50 A.D. here, returned seven years later.) The oldest part of the ramparts date from the 4th century A.D. and were built over fortifications dating from a much earlier period (Hellenistic period). One of the sides,

which was known as the sea wall — it stretched along the shore — was destroyed in the 19th century; only the White Tower now remains. Several of the former gates, including the one known as the Golden Gate, have also been pulled down to facilitate modern traffic. The oldest remaining gate is the Eski-Delik, which dates from the 4th century.

37. — *Thessalonika: the Church of St. George.* The church of St. George is probably one of the most important architectural achievements of Thessalonika, which is a veritable manual of Byzantine art and contains examples of every phase of its evolution. The church was originally a Roman building in the form of a rotunda, which the Christians turned into a church and the Turks into a mosque. After being restored to the Christians, it was finally secularized and submitted to the methodical examination of the architect F. Hebrard. The edifice is in the form of a circular hall with walls some 20 feet thick containing eight vaulted cradle niches to serve as windows. A dome roofs the entire building. Like the niches, the dome bears admirable mosaics with a gold background dating from the 5th century. The silhouettes of the saints are shown in a traditional attitude of prayer. The upper part of the cupola was probably destroyed a first time in the 10th century and a second in the 19th. The apse has paintings dating from the 15th century.

38. — *Thessalonika: the Crypt of St. Demetrius.* This crypt was discovered under the apse of the basilica of St. Demetrius after the terrible fire which destroyed the latter in 1917. St. Demetrius was considered the most beautiful church of Thessalonika. It was a 5th century Hellenistic basilica rebuilt in the 7th, with an atrium, a narthex, and five bays separated by rows of green marble colonnades. Unfortunately, hardly anything is left of the former mosaics other than those decorating the pillars at the entry of the apse, one of which shows St. Demetrius, the patron saint of the city.

39. — *Gulf of Nauplia.* Set in terraces on its rocky peninsula, Nauplia with its admirable gulf is one of the loveliest towns of Greece. The citadel is on the site of the acropolis of the ancient city and was rebuilt by the Venetians and the Turks. In ancient times, Nauplia was said to have been the work of Palamedes, the supposed inventor of the nautical art and the alphabet. In the middle of the 13th century, it became a possession of the dukes of Athens, who also gave themselves the title of Lords of Argos and Nauplia. William of Ville-

hardouin, who had conquered it, gave the city to his companion, Guy de la Roche. It was surrendered to the Venetians towards the end of the 14th century and was several times captured by the Turks.

40. — *Amphissa.* Destroyed by the Bulgarians, the ancient city of Amphissa owed its restoration to the Franks, who called it Salona. The barons of Amphissa were vassals of the king of Thessalonika. The castle, which was built by the Crusaders at the beginning of the 13th century and reinforced by the Catalans in the 14th, still mounts guard over the town. It has three enclosures of fine quadrangular bond, two towers, two gates, one of which is formed of three enormous blocks of stone, and finally a circular keep and two churches, one Frankish and the other Byzantine.

41. — *Kalamai.* William of Champlitte, the first prince of Morea, conquered the town of Kalamai as early a 1205 and Geoffrey of Villehardouin was proclaimed lord of Kalamata two years later. William II of Villehardouin, whose chronicles give such a magnificent picture of chivalry and who became for Goethe himself the embodiment of the perfect knight, was born and died here. The castle dates from the Frankish occupation and still overlooks the city around which the Venetians built walls in the 17th century.

42. — *The Castle of Klemutsi.* The castle of Klemutsi or Clermont (Clarence to the Venetians) is one of the most imposing feudal constructions of all Frankish Morea. Its Greek name means "tortoise shell" and is derived from the rocky promontory on which the fortress stands above the harbor, where the Genoese and Venetian trading vessels moored. The castle, which was also known as the "Château Tournois", was begun in 1219 and is one of the strongholds built to protect the coast road from Corinth to Kalamata, and Andravida, the Frankish capital. Although smaller than the Syrian castles, the fortresses of the princes of Morea give an impression of great power. They formed the backbone of the 13th century feudal society which brought new life to a region abandoned to a few peasants by the great landed aristocracy of Byzantine times, who had preferred to live at Constantinople.

43. — *The Great Hall of the Castle of Klemutsi.* This long vaulted gallery (150 feet by nearly 25) is in the hexagonal keep which stands in the center of the castle's crenelated walls with high towers. The fortress also contains the ruins of a chapel and the cistern

which ensured the water supply of the occupants. Klemutsi was captured in 1427 by Constantine Dragases and was dismantled by Ibrahim Pasha in the 19th century

44. — *Rhium*. The headlands of Rhium Andirrium guard the entry to the gulf of Corinth, not far from the shore of Missolonghi where Byron died. On Cape Rhiume lie the ruins of the castle of Morea from which the Turks watched the entry of the gulf. Nearby stands the town of Patras which, in the time of the Franks, was the seat of a barony and was later amalgamated with that of Mategriffon.

45. — *Livadia*. Situated on the crossroads of the gorges of Parnassus and the road to the north, Livadia was to become very important in the Middle Ages on account of its strategic position. The city has remained prosperous thanks to the cotton industry, (Cotton is grown to day on the site of the former Lake Copais, where the Frankish knights were defeated (by Catalan mercenaries in the 14th century.) A "kastro" or castle is now the only trace of the Frankish occupation. Under Turkish rule, Livadia became the second city of Greece (Athens remaining the first). Not far from Livadia was the spring of the oracle and waters of Lethe (forgetfulness), famous in classical times.

46. — *The Acrocorinth*. The Acrocorinth — or acropolis of Corinth — is situated on a scarped rock from which there is a wonderful view out over the Aegina and Salamis. In the distance are the hills of Atticus. The Acrocorinth was occupied by Roger II, the Norman king of Sicily, as early as the middle of the 12th century. In 1212, Villehardouin captured the stronghold, which was to pass through a number of hands in later years. The Acciaiuoli, the fabulous Florentine bankers, forced Robert of Tarente, one of the last princes of Morea, to yield them the seignory of Corinth. The Palaeologi captured the town in 1430, to be rapidly succeeded by the Turks, who were attacked in their turn by the knights of Malta. Corinth became part of Greece again only in 1821.

47. — *Walls of the Acrocorinth*. The extremely well preserved defences of the fortress of Corinth provide examples of all the different building techniques used in the construction of walls, from the 6th century B.C. to the Turkish invasion. The gate is defended by three successive enclosures linked together by ramps. The third contains whole sections of walls dating from classical times and a tower of the 4th century. Inside

the acropolis, there is the site of a temple to Aphrodite. In the 15th century, the inhabitants of Corinth took shelter in the fortress, where remains of their houses, chapels and barracks are still to be seen.

48. — *Foundation Letter of the Sainte-Chapelle by St. Louis (Louis IX of France)*. This letter dated January, 1246, was written by St. Louis and States the revenues of the chaplains and clerks of the chapel then being built within the walls of the king's palace in Paris to house the Holy Crown of Thorns, a piece of the True Cross, and holy relics from Constantinople.

The Latin Emperor of Constantinople, having found himself in financial difficulties, had pawned the Holy Crown of Thorns to Venetian merchants, and it was St. Louis who redeemed the relic. The Sainte-Chapelle, now regarded as a gem of Gothic art with its magnificent stained-glass windows, was the immense reliquary the king built for it. Two years later, St. Louis was to sail for the Holy Land and he had at this time begun to prepare for his Crusade. (Musée de l'Histoire de France, A E 2406).

49. — *Massacre of the Franks by Turkish Horsemen at Mansura*. The defeat of Mansura (a fortress guarding a canal on the road to Cairo) was the result of the rashness of St. Louis' brother, Robert of Artois, who covered the honor of capturing the stronghold with only the advance guard of which he was in command. The attack was made without the consent of the king, who had ordered Artois to wait for the main body of the expedition. The episode of the massacre is shown with much violence. The Turks, Mamelukes in the service of the sultan of Egypt, are armed with bows and large curved scimitars. This miniature comes from the 15th-century manuscript of the *Vie et Miracles de Saint-Louis*. (Bibl. nat., Français 2829, fol. 39 V°.).

50. — *Statue of St. Louis (13th century)*. This statue was ordered by Enguerrand of Marigny, the minister of Philippe le Bel, to decorate the chapel of his castle of Manneville, built at the end of the 13th century. Of polychrome stone, the statue is now in the church of Manneville (Eure, France).

51. — *Letter from the Emperor Frederick II to the Sicilians*. In November, 1246, the Emperor Frederick II, king of Jerusalem and Sicily, heard of the Crusade which the king of France was about to make. This letter to the Sicilians asks for the horses, arms and victuals he needed for his expedition.

The letter is sealed with a golden seal, over lakes of red silk. The sovereigns of the Holy Roman Empire, the Emperors of the Orient, and the city of Venice alone used the Golden Bull. One side of the seal in the photograph shows the emperor in majesty, while the other bears a picture of the port of Messina. (Musée de l'Histoire de France, A E III 101.)

52. — *Tomb of Isabella of Aragon.* The return of the crusade of St. Louis was a most woeful cortège. The king's body, together with that of his son, Jean-Tristan (who was born at Damietta), both victims of the plague, were escorted back to France by Charles of Anjou, the king's brother, by way of Africa, Sicily and Calabria. Hardly had the convoy set foot at Trapani, when Theobald, the king of Navarre and one of the royal suite, died. On reaching Cosenza, the young queen of France, Isabella, a princess of Aragon and wife of Philippe le Hardi, succumbed in her turn. (She had been thrown from her horse while crossing an icy torrent. The queen was six months pregnant at the time and the accident proved fatal.)

As was the custom of the period, her corpse was boiled and the flesh buried at Cosenza, while her bones were placed in the coffin holding the other dead and brought back to St. Denis by Charles of Anjou. Philippe le Hardi had a tomb built for her flesh near the altar of the Holy Apostles in the cathedral of Cosenza. A 13th-century masterpiece of sculpture, it is still in the north transept of the cathedral. It is said to be the work of a French artist.

53. — *The Desert of Negev.* The name of this desert situated in the southern part of the land of Israel means "dry." This was probably the region known to the Crusaders as *"Outre-Jourdain."* Its endless sand dunes, plains and mountains are extremely arid but of a great, though severe beauty. The temperature varies from 8⁰ F. in winter and 105⁰ F. in summer. The Israelis are now reclaiming the land which had been for so many hundreds of years the domain of the Bedouin nomads.

54. — *The Walls of Acre.* These walls guarding the town which was to become the last bastion of Frankish resistance — its fall in 1291 marked the end of the Latin kingdoms of the East — were said in the Middle Ages to be able to hold two chariots abreast. Though in ruins today, the walls are still one of the curiosities of the old city of Acre (present-day Akka).

Of the several towers along the ramparts (it takes about half an hour to walk all around the enclosure) only one actually dates from the 13th century: the Burj el Sultan tower, on the south corner. Its stones bear many masons' marks — crosses, triangles and letters — which indicated the amount of work done by each journeyman.

55 and 56. — *Seals of Fulk of Villaret and Villiers de l'Isle-Adam,* grand masters of the order of the Knights of St. John of Jerusalem (the Hospitallers), later the Knights of Rhodes.

57. — *Lindos: the Fortress.* Lindos, with its two harbors and grat rock of the acropolis, is one of the most important towns of Rhodes. The Knights of Rhodes built a fort here which was manned by a Greek garrison under the orders of twelve knights. Even to day, the town has 15th-century character and many of its Gothic houses are still intact. Of the castle, up to which lead long flights of steps, there remain the ruins of the commander's palace and a church to St John.

58. — *Rhodes: the Walls.* The walls of Rhodes, which date from the time of the knights, stand over a length of about two miles. They were built between 1478 and 1521. Surrounding them is a moat hollowed out of the rock, from 50 to 65 feet deep and from 100 to 150 feet wide, with a scarp and counterscarp.

59 and 60. — *Rhodes, the Former Infirmary and the Gate of Koskinu.* In the time of the knights, the infirmary, which could hold 100 beds, was a hall divided into two bays by seven octagonal pillars. Opposite the door stood a small chapel. The Knights of St. John of Jerusalem at Rhodes were ever faithful to their vocation of hospitallers. This hall now contains several tombstones of the knights, including that of the grand master, Pierre Cornaillon or Cornillon (1355).

The walls of Rhodes were divided into sections, each of which was entrusted to one of the tongues, or provinces, of the order. The north side of the walls, from the Tower of Naillac to the Amboise Gate (shown above), was in the charge of the knights of France. (The Amboise gate is most interesting from an architectural point of view. It has a draw bridge, a three-arched stone bridge, and two side turrets and still bears on the outside the shields of the order, including that of Aimery of Amboise, held by angels. It owes its name to the grand master of the order, the same Aimery of Amboise, who restored the gate in 1512.) The section of the walls between the Amboise Gate and St. George's bastion was entrusted to the Dalmatian tongue. From St. George's bastion to the Tower of Spain was the section belonging to the tongue of Auvergne. The section of the tongue of Aragon stretched from the Tower of Spain to St. Mary's Tower. From the latter there is now a magnificent view of the harbor and the coast. It was through a breach at this point that the Turks managed to enter the walls in 1522. From St. Mary's Tower to the Koskinu Gate, the ramparts were guarded by the tongue of England. The tongue of Provence was responsible for the section up to the bastion of Italy and the tongue of Italy from the Bastion of Italy as far as the Mill Gate. The tongue of Castille had charge of the remaining section along the trade harbor up to the Tower of Naillac.

61. — Rhodes: *the House of the Chaplains of France.*

62. — Rhodes: *the Hostel of France on the Rue des Chevaliers.* This hostel is to day one of the most interesting curiosities of Rhodes. It is on the main street of the former city and has remained unchanged since the 15th century. The inns or hostels of the various tongues of the order, that is to say their residences, are still to be seen along the street which leads to the citadel square, the highest point of the town where the palace of the grand masters stands. The latter was a splendid specimen of 14th-century military construction which the Turks made into a prison after the siege of 1522. Unfortunately, it was ruined by an explosion in 1856, though it has been restored since.

63. — *The Hostel of France at Rhodes.* Probably the finest of these inns or residences inhabited by the knights of the nations to which they belonged, the hostel of France is also the best preserved. The building may have been restored after the siege of 1480. Above the gate there is an inscription dating from 1492 which bears the name of the grand prior, Aimery of Amboise. The inn and chaplain's house of the tongue of France were restored in 1913-1914 by the French ambassador to Constantinople, Maurice Bompart. While St. John's cathedral, begun by the Hospitallers in 1310, is more Catalan in type than southern Italian, the influence of French Gothic art is to be found all over the island, not only in the ogival door of the little church close to the inn of France, but also in the larger buildings

such as the church of St. Catherine, which was later turned into a mosque (Kanturi Mosque).

64 and 65. — *Inner Courtyard and Chapel of the Knights' Hospital.* The Knights' Hospital, which was begun in 1440 and enlarged in 1480, was badly disfigured in the 19th century, when it was turned into a barracks. Restored during 1913-1918, it is now an archaeological museum where objects found during excavations made at Rhodes are to be seen. These include Mycenian objects from the necropolis of Jalyses, dating from the 8th century B.C., and objects of the classical and Byzantine epochs, represented in particular by a fine 6th-century mosaic. The tombstone of the knights and their chapel opening into the infirmary have already been mentioned above.

66, 67 and 68. — *The Palace of the Grand Masters; the Gate and the Inner Courtyard.* The palace is a magnificent rectangular edifice finished at the end of the 14th century. No other building illustrates quite as well the contribution of the Crusaders to Rhodes, as no other town provides so complete an example of a Frankish city in the East. The influence of the knights was so strong, indeed, that even in later years their methods of decorating remained in use at Rhodes, and Moslem techniques had the greatest difficulty in taking their place and have left few traces. Almost all the buildings of this period have a central courtyard with an open stairway set on pilasters. The grand masters came from all over western Europe and their constructions recall those of their homelands, making Rhodes a kind of résumé of 14th and 15th century western art.

69. — *The Return of the Crusader* (Chapel of the Greyfriars Monastery at Nancy, France). An admirable Romanesque sculpture of great pathos, this piece comes from the Benedictine Priory of Belval in the Vosges (northeastern France). It was transferred in the 19th century to the chapel of the Greyfriars of Nancy. It is generally thought to be the tombstone of Hugh 1st, Count of Vaudemont, who left for the Holy Land with Louis VII of France around 1147 and was for many years thought to be dead. His wife, Anne of Lorraine, refused to remarry, however, and patiently awaited his return, which took place, contrary to all hope, in 1163. The sculpture shows the knight being welcomed by his wife. He is wearing the cross on his shoulder and (such realism was rare at the period) his clothes are in rags.

ITINERARIES
OF THE
MAIN CRUSADES

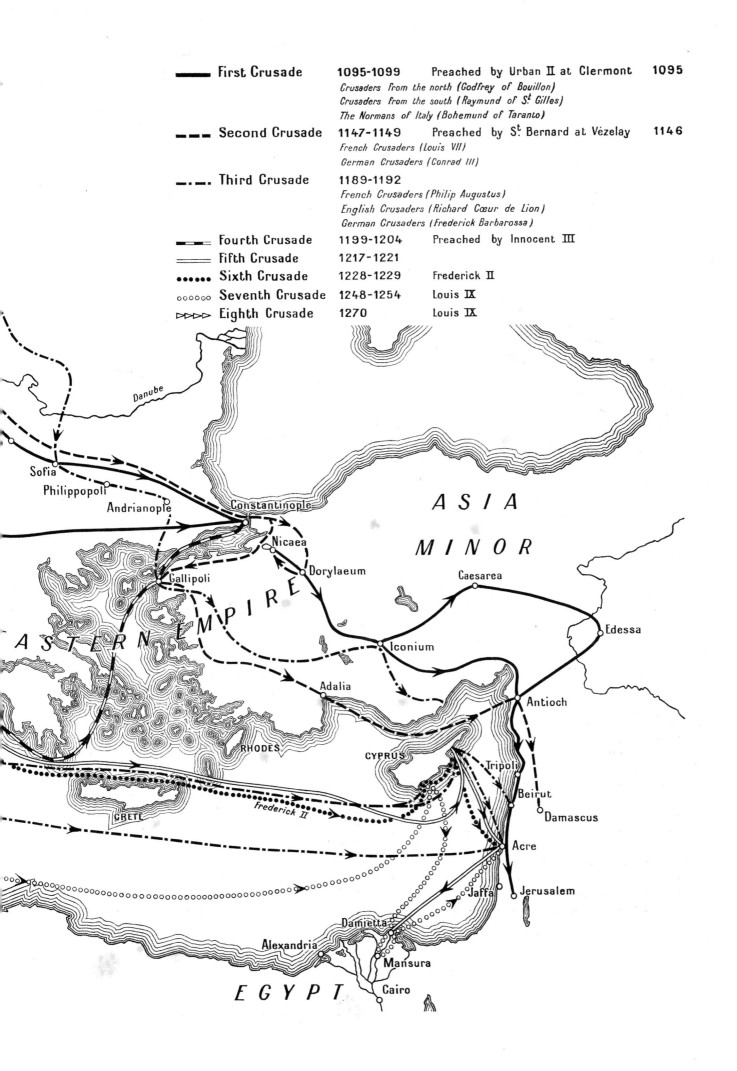

First Crusade 1095-1099 Preached by Urban II at Clermont 1095
Crusaders from the north (Godfrey of Bouillon)
Crusaders from the south (Raymund of St Gilles)
The Normans of Italy (Bohemund of Taranto)

Second Crusade 1147-1149 Preached by St Bernard at Vézelay 1146
French Crusaders (Louis VII)
German Crusaders (Conrad III)

Third Crusade 1189-1192
French Crusaders (Philip Augustus)
English Crusaders (Richard Cœur de Lion)
German Crusaders (Frederick Barbarossa)

Fourth Crusade 1199-1204 Preached by Innocent III
Fifth Crusade 1217-1221
Sixth Crusade 1228-1229 Frederick II
Seventh Crusade 1248-1254 Louis IX
Eighth Crusade 1270 Louis IX

Danube

Sofia
Philippopoli
Andrianople
Constantinople

ASIA

MINOR

Nicaea
Dorylaeum
Gallipoli

Caesarea

EASTERN EMPIRE

Iconium

Edessa

Adalia

Antioch

RHODES

CYPRUS

Tripoli

Beirut
Damascus

CRETE
Frederick II

Acre

Jaffa
Jerusalem

Damietta

Alexandria
Mansura

EGYPT
Cairo

COLORED PLATES

Pl. I. — *The Capture of Jerusalem* (manuscript). The miniature shows the storming of the walls of the Holy City on the 15th of July, 1099. At the top of the wheeled tower leading the way into Jerusalem stand Godfrey of Bouillon and the Lorrainese, to be recognized from their standards. After them come the Flemish, the Champenois, and the Catalans. Inside the walls, the artist has placed a series of pictures recalling all that the Holy City meant to the Christians: from left to right, the arrest of Christ and the kiss of Judas, Christ submitting to the outrages of the soldiers, Christ on his way to Calvary, the Crucifixion, and finally the burial of Jesus. To the right is a wheeled machine with a balance used to catapult stones against the walls. (Bibl. nat., Français 352, fol.V°. Beginning of the 14th century.)

Pl. II. — *Krak des Chevaliers*. This magnificent castle, the largest of those built by the Crusaders in Syria, stands on one of the main roads from the coast to the valley of the Orontes. Its position allowed the Franks to guard the famous "hollow of Homs," through which passed the caravans, and thus to regulate all the traffic going to the big Christian towns of Tortosa and Tripoli. The very fertile surrounding region supplied the castle. The Hospitallers settled here as early as 1142 and were to remain in occupation until 1271, or for nearly 130 years, in spite of repeated Moslem attacks. (The Moslems called the Krak "the bone in their throat.") Paul Deschamps, who has made the most complete study of this prodigious fortress, says that the progress made in the art of castle building during the 12th and 13th centuries could be studied solely from the Krak "so many and varied were the works undertaken by the knights, who were continually renewing or improving the defences of the fortress, where building seems never to have stopped." (*Le Krak des Chevaliers*, Paris, 1934, p. 112.) One day at noon, the knights of the Krak made a sortie to the camp of Nureddin, guarded only by the sentries at this hour. Armed from head to foot in spite of the overpowering heat, the Franks were thus able to surprise and overthrow the enemy at a single blow, pursuing the occupants as far as the shores of Lake Homs. This famous battle, known as that of the Boqa'a (1163), liberated the Krak from a siege which threatened to be terrible, for the Moslem forces were by far the more numerous.

Pl. III. — *View of the Capture of Constantinople*. This miniature illustrates one of the manuscripts of the *Voyage d'outre-mer* by Bertrandon de la Brogquière, a squire of Philippe le Bon, duke of Burgundy, who visited the city soon after the fall of the Byzantine Empire in 1432. (Bibl. nat., Français 9087, fol. 207 V°.)

Pl. IV. — *Mistra: Villehardouin's castle*. William of Villehardouin began this castle in 1249, after the capture of Malvoisie (Monemvasia). The stronghold, which dominates the entire region, was considered impregnable, but William was obliged to deliver it to Michel Palaeologus in exchange for his freedom, after being taken prisoner at Pelagonia (1259). This was as terrible a disaster to Frankish Greece as the defeat of Hattin had been to Syria. The Byzantines used the fortress to attempt to reconquer Laconia from the Franks. Sparta was to remain in the hands of the Villehardouins and be repopulated by them, however, opposite Byzantine Mistra. The keep of the castle, the tower close to the gate, and a few ruins of the chapel are all that is left of the Frankish period, the other parts of the castle having been rebuilt by the Turks.

Pl. V. — *Valley of the Alpheus.* Over this river, which was said in ancient fables to have been the son of Oceanus and Tethys, the Franks constructed a large six-arched stone bridge. On the heights over the valley, they built one of their most powerful castles at Karitaina. Later a Byzantine and then a Turkish possession, the castle still overlooks the valley.

Pl. VI. — *St. Louis Bearing the Holy Relics.* This stained-glass window (the fifteenth) in the Sainte-Chapelle in Paris shows the transporting of the relics by St. Louis (Louis IX of France) and his brother, Charles of Anjou, the Count of Provence.

Pl. VII. — *Rhodes: the Walls.* The island of Rhodes enjoyed great renown in ancient times. Pindar devoted one of his works to the celebration of its birth and the famous Colossus of Rhodes was one of the Seven Wonders of the World. The town itself was built to the plans of Hippodamus of Miletus, the most famous architect of the 5th century B.C. The island was also the refuge of the knights of St. John of

Jerusalem in the 14th century and for nearly two hundred years thereafter. Rhodes, which had shared the destiny of the Eastern Empire, of which it was a part, had been raided several times by the Saracens. Venetian merchants made it their base in 1082, after being granted a number of privileges by the emperor Alexis Comnenus. The Genoese took over the island in the 13th century and it was they who, in 1306, fifteen years after the fall of Acre, invited the Knights of St. John of Jerusalem who had up till then taken refuge at Cyprus. Having failed to persuade the emperor of Constantinople to give them the island as a fief, they captured it in 1309. They made it their base for operations against the Turks. Unlike the Templars, the Hospitallers never forgot their original aim, the assistance of the sick, all the while helping to defend the Holy Land. They were to organize a big fleet at Rhodes, which held out against the Turks until 1523. The siege lasted six months. The island was defended against the Turkish fleet (said to be carrying 100,000 men) by six hundred and fifty knights assisted by two hundred Genoese soldiers and the inhabitants. The knights had already successfully resisted two previous sieges (1444 and 1480). Rhodes was given back to Greece only in 1948.

Pl. VIII. — *A Pilgrims' Hostel Courtyard.* It was in the *collachium* (or quarter inhabited by the knights) that stood the inns or residences of each tongue, together with the palace of the grand master and St. John's cathedral. They all date from the 15th century, when they were restored if not actually built for the first time. The little Byzantine church of St. Mary, later the knights' cathedral, with its ogival vaults dating from the 13th century, should also be mentioned as one of the most interesting buildings of what is surely the most representative ensemble of western architecture in the Orient.

Imprimé en France - Héliogravure de S. A. P. H. O. - Typographie de E. PIGELET, Paris - N° 996.
Dépôt légal n° 877 - 3ᵉ trimestre 1959 - 1338 - I